MIM.

Highlights from the Musical Instrument Museum

Vielle à roue from France (page 134)

MIM.

Highlights from the Musical Instrument Museum

Library of Congress Cataloging-in-Publication Data Available

ISBN: 978-0-9853274-0-8

Karen Werner, *editor*
Jacqueline Byers, *photographer*
P.S. Studios, Inc., *design*

MIM is a museum in constant evolution. The instruments and exhibits featured in this book may not be on display in the future or may be displayed differently than they are depicted here.

theMIM.org

Cover image:
Bandoneón (p. 116)

Front endpaper image:
The group Umalali with *garawoun* drums. Punta Gorda, Belize, November 2011.

Back endpaper image:
Musicians performing on *donso ngoni* hunters' harps. Bamako, Mali, July 2006.

Back cover and facing-page images:
First row: *Sanza* (p. 31), *Garamut* (p. 85), *Rámpora* (p. 119)
Second row: National "Glenwood 95" (p. 160), *Morin khuur* (p. 70), "Mark VI" tenor saxophone (p. 142)

MIM®

Highlights from the Musical Instrument Museum

MUSICAL INSTRUMENT MUSEUM

Phoenix, Arizona

Bajo sexto from Michoacán, Mexico (page 164)

Contents

"BB-4 Baby Bass" from Washington, USA (page 160)

PRESIDENT'S FOREWORD

Most of my career has involved working as a university professor of cultural anthropology and participating in global research projects that, at the most basic level, were about getting people to understand one another. Cultures are powerful. Those who have spent their lives immersed in one set of beliefs and traditions often have great difficulty understanding those who have learned other behaviors and customs. At the Musical Instrument Museum (MIM), it gives me great pleasure that our guests take away from the experience something both simple and profound: an understanding that humans, at all times and in all places, have felt the need to express themselves through creating musical instruments and music. Despite all the elements that divide us—race, background, ethnicity, politics, religion—there is something that unites us: music as the language of the soul.

When I was asked to be the founding president and director of MIM, our founder, Bob Ulrich, and his friend, Marc Felix, had already established much of the vision that has directed our efforts since then. MIM would represent the musical instruments of every country in the world in a way that would be both entertaining and educational. Being inclusive, representing cultural diversity, and making the museum a fun place to visit regardless of age, ethnicity, or gender were extremely important to us.

From its inception, MIM was designed with the guest in mind. The experience begins with an inviting Sonoran desert landscape and a grand, welcoming courtyard. The building's architecture is timeless, complementing the surroundings and providing an open, cheerful environment. Instruments are exhibited in open displays so that guests can more easily appreciate their craftsmanship and beauty. Exhibits show musical ensembles from every nation and many territories of the world, and maps on each display allow guests to quickly locate an unfamiliar country. Most importantly, audio and video recordings of

> Despite all the elements that divide us—race, background, ethnicity, politics, religion— there is something that unites us: music as the language of the soul.

instruments being played in their cultural context bring these objects to life and help guests understand the crucial role music has played throughout all of the world's cultures and periods of human history. Instruments also come to life in the acoustically superb, three-hundred-seat MIM Music Theater, where renowned musicians from around the globe allow guests to literally listen to the world.

MIM was built in record time for a museum of this size and scope. It took less than five years, from the earliest concept to the opening in April 2010. The bulk of the collection, which now numbers more than fifteen thousand instruments and objects, was assembled in less than three years by a small group of curators and 125 expert consultants from around the world. A dedicated, hardworking museum team; exceptional architects, contractors, and professional consultants; and many enthusiastic volunteers collaborated to create this incredible institution.

This book highlights more than two hundred musical instruments from MIM's collection, offering an overview of the museum's scope and quality. Even when you cannot be present to hear their sounds and see them being played, we hope this sampling allows you to enjoy their variety, their craftsmanship, and their beauty, and reminds you of the central place held by music among all peoples of the world.

Billie (Bill) R. DeWalt, PhD
MIM President and Director

MIM.

Musical Instrument Museum

A Brief History of MIM

Rising gracefully from the Phoenix desert, the Musical Instrument Museum (MIM) is a significant addition to the international museum community. The world's first truly global music museum, MIM has collected more than fifteen thousand instruments and artifacts from every country in the world, approximately five thousand of which are displayed at any given time. What's more, most MIM exhibits include high-quality audio/video recordings that allow guests to see and hear the instruments being played in their authentic native context.

MIM was founded by Robert J. Ulrich, chairman emeritus and former CEO of Target Corporation. A museum enthusiast and avid collector of African art, Ulrich came up with the idea for MIM in conjunction with a close friend, the noted African art dealer and author Marc Felix, after the two visited the storied Musical Instruments Museum in Brussels, Belgium. Their vision was to create a museum that celebrates the splendid diversity of music and musical instruments from every country in the world.

"The goal was to illuminate what is unique about cultures, and also what is shared and universal," says Ulrich. By using state-of-the-art audiovisual technology to show the instruments being played in their original cultural contexts and delivering the sound of these instruments through high-quality headphones, MIM would provide a world-class, one-of-a-kind guest experience.

One of the first steps in realizing that vision was to create an advisory Curatorial Council with members selected from the Smithsonian Institution, the Metropolitan Museum of Art in New York, the Minneapolis Institute of Arts, and the University of South Dakota's National Music Museum. Later additions to the council came from the Musée de la musique in Paris and the Museum of Fine Arts in Boston. The Royal Museum for Central Africa in Tervuren, Belgium was also a major contributor and partner in this process.

In March 2007, Billie (Bill) R. DeWalt, PhD, was recruited as MIM's founding president and director. A cultural anthropologist, Distinguished Service

MIM officially opened its doors on April 24, 2010, and immediately became recognized as a fun, guest-friendly, worldwide tourist destination.

Professor of Public and International Affairs, past director of the Center for Latin American Studies at the University of Pittsburgh, and former director of Carnegie Museum of Natural History in Pittsburgh, DeWalt began assembling a team of outstanding museum professionals, including five initial curators who brought varied backgrounds in musicology, ethnomusicology, and organology to MIM.

Following the purchase of a twenty-acre site in north Phoenix, MIM established a temporary headquarters in nearby Tempe, Arizona, in September 2007. Five months later—on February 6, 2008—a groundbreaking ceremony marked the start of construction of the award-winning 200,000-square-foot building that now houses MIM's collection, galleries, music theater, recording studio, conservation laboratory, café, museum store, and offices.

In early 2008, MIM acquired its first historically significant collection of 1,200 American, European, and world instruments, dating from the seventeenth through twentieth centuries, from Claremont University Consortium's Kenneth G. Fiske Museum at the Claremont Colleges in Southern California. Building on this foundation, MIM's curatorial team and 125 short-

Orientation Gallery

and long-term consultants have traveled the world collecting instruments and commissioning new instruments from noted makers.

MIM officially opened its doors on April 24, 2010, and immediately became recognized as a fun, guest-friendly, worldwide tourist destination. The recipient of numerous awards and accolades for its architecture, exhibits, and economic-development impact, MIM has created an exciting musical and cultural experience for guests, showcasing instruments from around the world. Exhibits for every country in the world are featured, along with exhibits that offer an insider's view of how some instruments are made, how they are played, or the varied contexts in which they are used.

MIM is committed to constantly evolve and change by improving its collection and rotating its exhibits so guests who return again and again will always see something new. The museum will also increasingly enhance its reputation as a research institution, becoming a destination for musicians, scholars, and others who can make effective use of its global collections. "The unique global perspective of our collection, its breadth, and depth allows us to make connections between countries and cultures that have never before been expressed in a museum setting," says DeWalt.

Music is something all humans share. It is a source of beauty and comfort, a means to give voice to joy and sorrow, and a powerful force for bringing people together. MIM celebrates music as all of these things, providing musical novices and experts, tourists and scholars alike a chance to see, hear, and feel the powerful and uniting force of music in an entirely new way.

MIM's curatorial team and 125 short- and long-term consultants have traveled the world collecting instruments and commissioning new instruments from noted makers.

Orientation Gallery

Target Gallery

Each instrument at MIM was selected for its fine construction, its special provenance, its cultural significance, its association with a notable performer, or for the reputation of its maker.

Building the Collection

MIM's distinctive global collection comprises instruments, artifacts, costumes/regalia, and audio and video recordings. The museum's curators, in consultation with distinguished musicologists and other experts, traveled the world, occasionally venturing into quite remote and turbulent regions, to collect instruments and to document indigenous cultures.

Fender Guitar Exhibit

MIM's distinctive global collection comprises instruments, artifacts, costumes/regalia, and audio and video recordings.

MIM's **Africa** gallery displays instruments and artifacts from sub-Saharan nations. Here guests discover the royal court music of Rwanda and Burundi, the spirit-calling drums of Benin, an ivory trumpet used ceremonially by a female secret society in Sierra Leone, and large zoomorphic slit drums used for communication in the Democratic Republic of the Congo. The **Middle East / North Africa** gallery continues to explore musical traditions in countries such as Egypt, Turkey, Syria, and Israel.

The **Asia** gallery features instruments from countries in four sub-galleries devoted to the regions of East Asia, South Asia, Southeast Asia, and Central Asia and the Caucasus. Here museum guests can see a Javanese gamelan orchestra and MIM's re-creation of an Indonesian gong workshop. The adjacent **Oceania** gallery immerses guests in music of the Pacific, showcasing the instruments and cultures of many island groups.

The **Latin America** gallery contains instruments and ensembles displayed in three sub-galleries: South America, Central America and Mexico, and the Caribbean. Here MIM guests can see many

Each instrument was selected for its fine construction, its special provenance, its cultural significance, its association with a notable performer, or for the reputation of its maker. The collection is presented in **Geographical Galleries** that focus on major world regions as well as in a special **Artist Gallery**, which features instruments played by some of the world's leading musicians.

7

Africa Gallery

instruments that are common to several countries, as well as some that are unique to specific areas and peoples. Highlights include an exhibit devoted to music-filled Afro-Caribbean processions and religious festivals; a re-created Bolivian Jesuit mission (c. 1800) with instruments by celebrated maker Ricardo Massun; and an exhibition showing the dancing masqueraders and "musickers" featured in holiday folk dramas throughout the English-speaking Caribbean.

In the **Europe** gallery, guests encounter a French revolutionary military parade, a rustic Catalonian kitchen, and a contemporary Ukrainian wedding procession. Other highlights include a mid-nineteenth-century symphony orchestra exhibit, a Bohemian viola d'amore (c. 1725), and an early synthesizer (c. 1947) called an *ondioline,* which was invented by Georges Jenny.

At MIM, a guest's close physical encounter with instruments is enhanced by state-of-the-art audio and video technologies that bring to life the sounds and sights of the instruments on display.

In contrast to the other Geographical Galleries, exhibits in the **United States / Canada** gallery are organized by musical genre. Ranging from hip hop to Sousa bands, the displays in the United States / Canada gallery explore traditional and popular sounds from the Arctic to the Mexican border. Guests can observe the diverse array of instruments that shaped the North American musical landscape, including the Appalachian dulcimer, sousaphone, ukulele, and electric guitar. The music of native peoples in the United States and Canada is highlighted in displays that explore old and new musical practices, with instruments such as the water drum, the Native American flute, and the Apache fiddle. Special exhibits focus on iconic American musical-instrument manufacturers, including Fender, Martin, and Steinway.

Finally, MIM's ever-changing **Artist Gallery** displays musical instruments linked to world-renowned musicians and music innovators such as John Lennon, Elvis Presley, Carlos Santana, Eric Clapton, Paul Simon, and Dick Dale, as well as concert video, photographs, performance outfits, and other special items.

About the Technology

At MIM, a guest's close physical encounter with instruments is enhanced by state-of-the-art audio and video technologies that bring to life the sounds and sights of the instruments on display. MIM's galleries utilize advanced wireless headsets and high-resolution video screens, enabling guests simultaneously to see instruments, hear their sounds, and observe them being used in their original contexts—performances that are often as spectacular as the instruments themselves.

Every guest who enters MIM receives one of approximately 1,800 Sennheiser guidePORT™ compact receiver/headphone units that MIM has available to guide visitors throughout the museum. These headphones—completely automatic and providing excellent audio quality—deliver the soundtrack for videos located at hundreds of sites around the museum.

As guests approach a display, identifiers hidden in the exhibits cue the audio guides to tap into audio signals that are synchronized with the video displays. In this way, while guests see the actual instruments up close, they also enjoy the unique sounds and sights of each musical culture that go with them. "You get an idea from the video of how to play the instrument," DeWalt says. "Is it plucked? Is it bowed? Is it struck? And you also get a sense of what the music is all about."

While guests see the actual instruments up close, they also enjoy the unique sounds and sights of each musical culture that go with them.

Conservation Lab

9

Phoenix, by Louis Halleux
(Made possible by a gift from the Susanne and Gary Tobey Family Foundation)

MIM's distinctive architecture evokes the topography of the Southwest.

Architecture in Harmony

The 200,000-square-foot museum and grounds feature two floors of galleries, the MIM Music Theater and recording studio, a conservation laboratory, a classroom, two courtyards, the MIM Café and Coffee Shop, and the Museum Store. Designed by award-winning architect Rich Varda and a team from RSP Architects of Phoenix and Minneapolis, MIM's distinctive architecture evokes the topography of the Southwest. Built by Ryan Companies of Phoenix and Minneapolis, the building utilizes exquisite materials and was constructed by expert craftspeople from a wide variety of building trades.

The museum's façade features richly grained Indian sandstone that complements the surrounding desert colors of Arizona. As guests approach the building, they pass through a landscape of native plants designed by Ten Eyck Landscape Architects of Phoenix and Austin, Texas. The adjacent courtyard features *Phoenix,* a rotating bronze sculpture of blended instrumental forms by Belgian artist Louis Halleux, as well as a series of "streams" that give the space a serene appeal.

The two-story museum structure includes 80,000 square feet of gallery space, with a 450-foot-long river-like corridor called "El Río" that forms the spine of the museum, links the central atrium to the interior galleries, and offers

GUITARS
Many Forms, Many Countries

Guitar Exhibit

The award-winning Café at MIM

Museum Store

changing views of the space. Beautiful patterns in the exterior sandstone suggest the geological striations of the Arizona landscape, while the building itself connotes shapes common to musical instruments. Diffused daylight through skylights and windows reminiscent of piano keys illuminates the galleries.

In addition to Guest Service, the Artist Gallery, the Café at MIM, the Museum Store, and the Family Center, MIM's first floor houses the Orientation Gallery, the Conservation Lab, and the Guitar Gallery. Meanwhile, also on the first floor, the Target Gallery hosts special temporary exhibitions and touring shows, while the Mechanical Music Gallery contains instruments designed to play on their own. Next

The building utilizes exquisite materials and was constructed by expert craftspeople from a wide variety of building trades.

door is the Experience Gallery, a hands-on space where guests can play an array of instruments, including drums, a Javanese gamelan, *sanzas* (thumb pianos), a theremin, and Little Martin guitars. This gallery is adjacent to a classroom that houses special workshops and other educational programs.

11

Guests study the mosaic map of MIM's Geographical Galleries.

A view of the entrance to the Asia Gallery.

The museum and its collection beckon people from every nation and walk of life to be amazed by the beauty and diversity of the world's musical instruments and cultures.

Drawing guests upstairs is a dynamic spiral staircase that features at its base a unique mosaic floor map of the world created with multicolored stones from around the globe. The second floor, also accessible by escalator and elevator, is devoted to MIM's extensive core collections and houses the museum's vast Geographical Galleries. Cherrywood doorway treatments signal the transitions between geographical regions.

Kaigal-ool Khovalyg

Jordin Sparks

Tommy Emmanuel

At the MIM Music Theater you can, quite literally, listen to the world.

Spanning both floors of the museum is the three-hundred-seat Music Theater. Designed with spacious seating and superb state-of-the-art acoustics, the intimate hall is a premier venue for performances, films, and seminars. An adjacent recording studio allows MIM to capture live recordings of many of the performances in the theater. At the MIM Music Theater you can, quite literally, listen to the world.

Together, the museum and its collection beckon people from every nation and walk of life to be amazed by the beauty and diversity of the world's musical instruments and cultures, and to be enriched by their sounds and their stories.

Africa Gallery

AFRICA (Sub-Saharan)

Angola
Benin
Botswana
Burkina Faso
Burundi
Cameroon
Cape Verde
Central African Republic
Chad
Comoros
Congo, Democratic Republic of the
Congo, Republic of the
Djibouti
Equatorial Guinea
Eritrea
Ethiopia
Gabon
Gambia
Ghana
Guinea
Guinea-Bissau
Ivory Coast
Kenya
Lesotho
Liberia
Madagascar
Malawi
Mali
Mauritius
Mozambique
Namibia
Niger
Nigeria
Rwanda
São Tomé and Príncipe
Senegal
Seychelles
Sierra Leone
Somalia
South Africa
South Sudan
Sudan
Swaziland
Tanzania
Togo
Uganda
Zambia
Zimbabwe

Africa is a land of varied geography, from mountains to rainforests to desert plains. It is a continent rich in both natural resources and musical traditions. The nearly 50 exhibits in MIM's Africa gallery showcase the importance of music in a diverse array of African cultures.

If there is such a thing as a soul of Africa, it may be found in the vibrant music that permeates the continent. MIM's Africa collection currently contains nearly two thousand musical instruments. Along with videos, photographs, and other contextual materials, these instruments provide guests a unique opportunity to enjoy Africa's varied musical arts and traditions.

The African rhythms, melodies, and sounds that we enjoy internationally today originate from a large and diverse repertoire of traditional instruments that are still part of the everyday lives of numerous African peoples. These instruments include drums, xylophones, *sanzas,* gongs, bells, rattles, and bullroarers. Whistles, trumpets, and flutes, as well as musical bows, fiddles, harps, and guitars, are also included.

The Kenya exhibit features horns and flutes from the country's pastoralist cultures, as well as lyres, fiddles, and drums from peoples inhabiting the west and coastal areas.

The African rhythms, melodies, and sounds that we enjoy internationally today originate from a large and diverse repertoire of traditional instruments that are still part of the everyday lives of numerous African peoples.

String instruments such as harps, existing in many forms throughout Africa, are choice instruments for traditional storytellers, such as the Mande griots of West Africa. Similarly, Central African "praise singers" recount their oral histories accompanied by highly refined harps. From areas of Central Africa to eastern and southern parts of the continent, *sanzas* (or thumb pianos, which go by different names in different African countries) became the preferred instrument for itinerant performers who traveled long distances to entertain, impart peoples' histories, and disseminate "the news," sometimes working as emissaries for important chiefs.

Finely crafted trumpets were used to accompany royal processions during the times of the different African kingdoms. Instrument makers from the Kingdom of Benin (present-day Nigeria) and the Kongo (today's Angola, Republic of the Congo, and the Democratic Republic of the Congo) created trumpets carved in ivory—some including symbolic motifs and scenes involving humans, animals, and nature.

African diviners, past and present, have employed a number of musical instruments to draw the attention of the tutelary spirits who aid humans with their problems. Rattles, bells, miniature xylophones, whistles, and drums are all used to summon a spirit's assistance. Once a diviner has determined the cause of a particular problem, and a potential cure, other instruments may be called into play to cure a sickness or redress an adversity.

Africa's predominant musical instrument is the drum. Well-known drum types include the West African *djembe,* a single-headed, goblet-shaped drum played with both hands, and the so-called "talking drum," an hourglass-shaped, double-headed drum held under the arm to apply pressure to tension strings, creating different tones while striking a head with a curved drumstick.

The Baule of Ivory Coast and the Fon of Benin produce exemplary, tall, single-headed drums that are commonly decorated with artistic imagery. Some of these drums are conceived with human anatomical details. Indeed, drums are often perceived as metaphors for the human body (particularly female), with the sounds understood as "voices" from the spirit realm. Others are part of drumming ensembles in which each drum's sounds/beats complement the others.

Enduring legacies of Africa in today's global music can be found in jazz, soul, gospel, blues, samba, salsa, reggae, and even rock and tango (to name a

The Democratic Republic of the Congo exhibits highlight the country's diverse musical instruments, divided under thematic titles such as "hierarchy," "communication," "narrative," and "ritual." The exhibits include approximately 100 notable objects on loan from the Royal Museum for Central Africa in Tervuren, Belgium.

few). In the late twentieth century, some of these genres "returned" to Africa through recordings, radio broadcasts, and performances of international musicians, many of whom played alongside African musicians in countries such as Mali, Congo, and South Africa. African musicians have, in turn, performed in Europe, the United States, and elsewhere, and have become global artists themselves. This cross-pollination has led to new terms like "world beat" and to new hybrid genres of music, such as African pop (Afropop), that combine African influences with others from around the world.

Instruments
of the
Africa Gallery

Buru (side-blown trumpet)

**BAMANA PEOPLE,
MALI, EARLY 20TH c.**
Wood
35¼ x 4 in.

Among the Bamana, "power associations" harvest and manage *nyama,* the energy or force of all things in the universe. This trumpet belongs in that context as an instrument that directs, through its sound, those energies toward specific goals.

Sinbi (harp)

MANINKA PEOPLE, MALI, 1980
Gourd, wood, bamboo, animal skin, rope, metal
Bala Guimba Diakite, maker
45⁵⁄₁₆ x 11¼ x 15⁹⁄₁₆ in.

The *sinbi* is a traditional seven-stringed harp used by Mande-speaking peoples of West Africa. It is played for hunters, and it is believed that a hunter originally discovered the instrument in an encounter with a bush spirit.

Goblet drum

BAGA PEOPLE, GUINEA, EARLY 20TH c.
Wood, cowhide
50 x 16 in.
*Loan courtesy of Royal Museum for Central Africa,
Tervuren, Belgium (MO.1961.26.1)*

Large and colorful drums with figurative
supports are played in Baga male and
female initiations. The maternity figure
carved as a structural element for this
drum symbolically reinforces the theme
of birth, rebirth, and continuity, central to
initiation rituals.

Side-blown trumpet
MENDE PEOPLE, SIERRA LEONE, MID-20TH c.

Ivory

24 x 4 in.

Loan courtesy of Royal Museum for Central Africa, Tervuren, Belgium (MO.1973.43.4)

This ivory trumpet's finial, in the form of an anthropomorphic head, may represent a Sande society helmet mask, the only wooden mask worn by women in Africa. The trumpet may have been used ceremonially in Sande female initiations among the Mende.

Atungblan (single-headed cylindrical drum)
BAULE PEOPLE, IVORY COAST, EARLY 20TH c.

Wood, animal skin

82½ x 12 in.

This long drum, also called *kiln kpli,* includes carved human and zoomorphic heads, and a serpent that wraps around the instrument's body. The drum symbolically bridges the world of humans with wilderness and ancestral spirits. These aspects of the Baule universe are engaged through music and performances during important ceremonies.

Gyil (gourd-resonated xylophone)

DAGARA PEOPLE, FALU, UPPER WEST REGION, GHANA, 1990
Wood, gourd, rope
Ba Wua, maker
68 x 29 x 31½ in.

The 18-bar *gyil* xylophone features a number of gourd resonators underneath. These are carefully tuned to correlate with the tonal languages of the region. The instrument's "voice" may be featured in solo performances, or as part of an ensemble that includes a secondary xylophone and a few other instruments.

Single-headed cylindrical drum

FON PEOPLE, BENIN, MID-20TH c.
Wood, animal skin, paint
58 x 22 in.

In parts of Africa, drums are sometimes carved to imitate details of the female body. This is meant to metaphorically correlate concepts of human fertility with the idea of a fertile instrument and sound. This reinforces the themes of fruitfulness and regeneration, important to drum-led rituals and ceremonies that mark human transitions, such as initiations and funerals.

Ìlù (goblet drum)

YORÙBÁ PEOPLE, ÈKÌKÌ, NIGERIA, EARLY 20TH c.
Wood, animal skin
32 x 10 in.; 29 x 10 in.

The birth rate for twins among the Yorùbá is about four times higher than in the rest of the world. This pair of drums was probably used in rituals to honor the Yorùbá deity of twins, Òrìṣà Ìbejì.

Fly whisk

**BAMILEKE PEOPLE,
CAMEROON, EARLY 20ᵀᴴ c.**
Wood, textile, animal hair, beads
54½ x 9 x 12 in.

Bell

**BAMILEKE PEOPLE,
CAMEROON, EARLY 20ᵀᴴ c.**
Iron, textile, beads
17¾ x 4 x 4 in.

Seated figure

**BAMILEKE PEOPLE,
CAMEROON, EARLY 20ᵀᴴ c.**
Wood, textile, beads
21½ x 8¾ x 9 in.

These beaded objects, including an
iron bell with an anthropomorphic handle,
are part of a set of items that served as
emblems of rank for an important chief.
Iron bells, meant to be played with sticks,
are commonly found throughout Africa
in important settings, to provide musical
accompaniment or demarcate, through
sound, ceremonial steps or actions.

Pluriarc

**BAMILEKE PEOPLE,
CAMEROON, EARLY 20TH c.**
Wood, wire
29 x 7½ x 9 in.

Pluriarcs are particularly
rich plucked instruments
with multiple musical bows
projecting from a resonator.
This fine example includes
fish and turtle motifs,
part of the repertoire of
symbolic themes featured
in a performer's lyrics.

Bell

**SANGO PEOPLE, CENTRAL
AFRICAN REPUBLIC, MID-20TH c.**
Wood
14 x 9 x 4¼ in.
Gift of Robert J. Ulrich

Collected from a Sango man
from the Central African
Republic, this anthropomorphic
wooden bell may originate
from the Democratic Republic
of the Congo (DRC), further
south. Related bells have been
documented among the Zande,
and used to create sound
accompaniment for a king's
gestures and actions.

Tom (lyre)

SHILLUK (CHOLLO) PEOPLE, NEAR MALAKAL, SOUTH SUDAN, 20TH c.
Wood, metal, cowhide, beads, textile, shells
43 x 34½ x 6 in.

This lyre was collected near the banks of the White Nile, in what is today Africa's youngest country, South Sudan. The Sudanese interaction with Egypt—and by extension Greece—since antiquity, resulted in a bridging of cultures, which made the lyre a treasured musical instrument.

Gugu (slit drum)

BARAMBO PEOPLE, UELE PROVINCE, DEMOCRATIC REPUBLIC OF THE CONGO (DRC), EARLY 20TH c.
Wood
77¾ x 30⅜ x 29⅛ in.
Acquired in honor of Robert J. Ulrich through the generosity of the Target Corporation executive team

Important chiefs in the northern DRC kept large wooden slit drums to communicate long-distance—village-to-village—with their subjects. This example, conceived in the form of a buffalo, served to correlate the animal's attributes of strength and endurance with a chief's abilities.

Kundi (arched harp)

ZANDE PEOPLE, UELE REGION, DEMOCRATIC REPUBLIC OF THE CONGO (DRC), LATE 19TH–EARLY 20TH c.
Wood, fiber
33¹⁄₁₆ x 9¹⁄₁₆ x 17⅛ in.
Loan courtesy of Royal Museum for Central Africa, Tervuren, Belgium (MO.0.0.562)

Harps from the northern DRC and South Sudan are among the most elegant and refined musical instruments of Africa. Conceived with full figures or with figurative heads, the images may have once honored prominent individuals.

Did You Know?

The term *kundi*, used for these harps among the Zande, is associated with "happiness."

Sanza

**ZANDE PEOPLE, DEMOCRATIC REPUBLIC
OF THE CONGO (DRC), EARLY 20TH c.**
Wood, bamboo, rubber
27½ x 7 x 5½ in.
*Loan courtesy of Royal Museum for Central Africa,
Tervuren, Belgium (MO.0.0.22548)*

This thumb piano takes the form of a
freestanding figure, probably an ancestral
representation. The fact that, in play, the
"body" of the figure creates music may be
a metaphor for fertile sound and fruitful
communication among humans and with
the realm of ancestors.

Curator's Note

The cross motif is an ancient symbol of empowerment that predates its association with Christianity among the Kongo people.

Side-blown trumpet

KONGO PEOPLE, DEMOCRATIC REPUBLIC OF THE CONGO (DRC), EARLY TO MID-16TH c.

Ivory
18 x 1½ in.
Gift of Marc Leo Felix

This ivory trumpet is the oldest musical instrument in MIM's African collection. It is estimated to have been in use in the 16th century, when Afonso I ruled (1509–1542) as the first Christian monarch of the Kongo Kingdom. The trumpet shows a deep patina from old age.

Slit drum

NDENGESE PEOPLE, KASAÏ PROVINCE, DEMOCRATIC REPUBLIC OF THE CONGO (DRC), MID-20TH c.
Wood
28½ x 12¼ x 14 in.
Gift of Robert J. Ulrich

The Ndengese are known for intricate designs and patterns in their carvings, textiles, and basketry. The motifs may be read as symbols or as conceptual arrangements reflecting order or spatial relations. The high/low-relief decorations on this drum vary the thickness of its wall, which creates different tones when it is struck with beaters.

Sanza

SONGYE PEOPLE, DEMOCRATIC REPUBLIC OF THE CONGO (DRC), EARLY 20TH c.
Gourd, wood, iron
13½ x 17½ in.

Thumb pianos are commonly used to musically accompany praise songs and storytelling in Central Africa. This example retains its very large (and fragile) gourd resonator, which significantly amplifies the instrument's sounds.

Begana (lyre)

ETHIOPIA, 20ᵀᴴ c.
Wood, cowhide
56 x 23¾ x 8 in.

Painted manuscripts from the
Ethiopian Coptic Church feature
the biblical King David playing a
begana lyre similar to this one.
The *begana,* with a square box
resonator and ornate arms and
crossbar, is said to have been a
gift of God to King David so he
could perform religious songs.

Kor (bell)

SOMALI PEOPLE, SOMALIA, 1992
Wood, sisal fibers, metal
Hagadera Wood Carving Group, maker
8½ x 6 x 7 in.

Somali *kor* are made to be worn by lead camels to alert the herd when it is time to move. Carving such bells is an elaborate task that reflects Somali appreciation for an animal that is essential to their livelihoods. The bells are also used to accompany praise songs dedicated to their livestock.

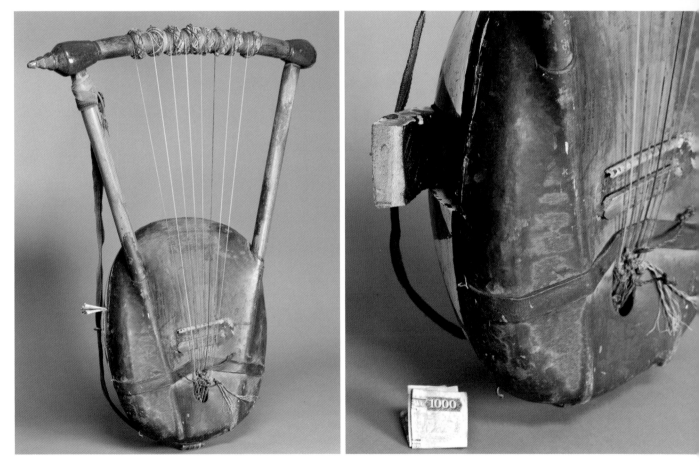

Nyatiti (lyre)

LUO PEOPLE, ALEGO VILLAGE, NYANZA PROVINCE, KENYA, 1976
Wood, cowhide, sisal fibers
Angira Korondo, maker
25½ x 22¾ x 9 in.

This lyre was owned by a renowned Luo musician, Apiyo Atieno, from the same province in Kenya and of the same ethnic background as President Barack Obama's father. It features a small door and compartment for depositing money collected during performances.

Side-blown trumpet

ZARAMO PEOPLE, TANZANIA, 19ᵀᴴ c.
Ivory, wood, animal skin
41 x 4½ in.
Gift of Robert J. Ulrich

This instrument incorporates a short
segment of an ivory tusk with a carved
hollow wooden extension to create a
long, side-blown trumpet. The materials
added to join the parts—including
an animal skin—make this trumpet's
construction particularly interesting.

Ondjembo erose (trumpet)

HIMBA PEOPLE, NAMIBIA, MID-20ᵀᴴ c.
Gemsbok horn, beeswax
26¾ x 4¼ in.

The Himba, a sub-group of the Herero
in Angola and Namibia, traditionally
are semi-nomadic herders managing
mainly cattle. Relatively rare in
collections, their trumpets are used
for communication and to herd cattle
as well as to accompany praise songs
celebrating the Himba way of life.

Afri-can guitar (plucked lute)

CAPE TOWN, SOUTH AFRICA, 2009
Metal, plastic
Township Guitars, maker
36¼ x 7¾ x 6¼ in.

South African Graeme Wells (1961–2008) designed his first electric guitar trying to improve technically upon those commonly found throughout Africa made from recycled materials. His tin-can guitars quickly gained commercial popularity, ending up in the hands of South African musicians and collected by groups such as UB40. Wells's guitars are now produced in South Africa by Township Guitars.

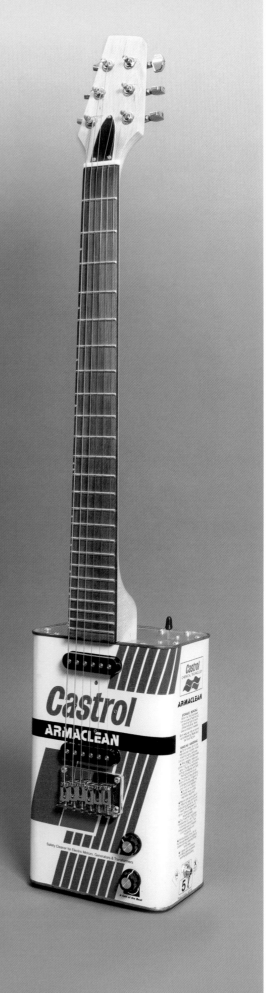

The Ghana and Togo exhibits showcase musical traditions as a source of ethnic, as well as national, identity and pride. Featured in the displays are instruments from the Ashanti, Ewe, Fanti, and Ga peoples of Ghana and of the Ewe, Fon, and Hausa peoples of Togo.

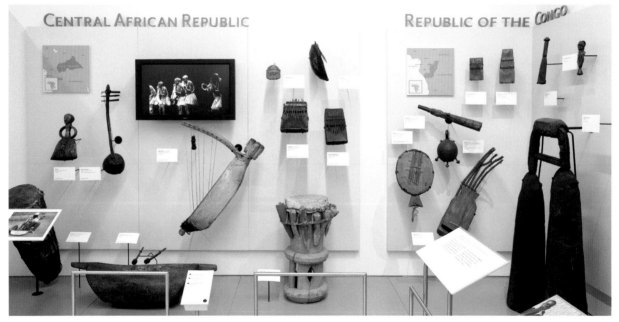

The Central African Republic and Republic of the Congo exhibits illustrate shared instruments from these regions, such as finely conceived arched harps, pluriarcs, *sanzas*, trumpets, bells, and different drum types.

(right) **The Guinea and Guinea-Bissau exhibits** include a masquerade and musical instruments such as the kora harp-lute, which is played by musicians who also serve as oral historians.

GUINEA

GUINEA-BISSAU

Middle East / North Africa Gallery

MIDDLE EAST

Bahrain
Iran
Iraq
Israel
Jordan
Kuwait
Lebanon
Oman
Qatar
Saudi Arabia
Syria
Turkey
United Arab Emirates
Yemen

NORTH AFRICA

Algeria
Egypt
Libya
Mauritania
Morocco
Tunisia

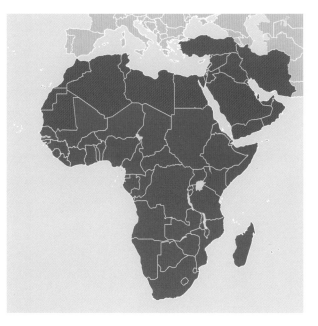

The Middle East and North Africa exhibits at MIM invite guests to experience an assortment of music and cultures. The gallery represents a region that extends along Africa's Sahara Desert, across the Red and eastern Mediterranean Seas, to the countries surrounding the Persian Gulf.

The peoples of the Middle East and North Africa have been in contact for thousands of years. As a result, through the centuries the area has seen the development of great centers of learning, rich commerce, and thriving traditions of scholarship, poetry, and music. The Middle East and North Africa, although distinct, are represented together at MIM because they are linked musically by shared traditions and streams of influence.

The Syria exhibit features the beauty and artistry of instruments such as the *'ūd* and the *qānūn* zither.

Countries in the Middle East share much of their urban and rural music, while also maintaining their own distinct local flavors.

Much of the music in North Africa harks back to Arab roots, as do characteristic instruments such as the *'ūd, nāy, qanun,* and *darbukka.* The Morocco, Tunisia, and Algeria exhibits highlight Arab-Andalusian music, a fusion of Arab traditions with African and Berber influences that is very popular throughout the region. The Egypt exhibit also presents Arab influence; great Egyptian performers and composers in the twentieth century have blended Arab and European instruments in an urban context to create music that remains a standard today.

Countries in the Middle East share much of their urban and rural music, while also maintaining their own distinct local flavors. Iran draws from its Persian heritage to create a unique melodic vocabulary. Syria, Iraq, and Turkey have enduring traditions of their own with Sufi mysticism as a predominant influence. Israel is known worldwide for symphonic performance and popular groups that combine Arab, Jewish, and European musical styles.

Among the instruments of the Middle East, the '*ūd* stands out for its longevity, its iconic appeal, and its influence abroad. From ancient origins in Iran and Iraq, this pear-shaped lute spread throughout western Asia and, with the expansion of Islam across northern Africa, it circulated from Iraq to Turkey to Morocco and all points between. Trade along the Silk Road took the '*ūd* eastward, inspiring instruments of similar shape and structure in China and Japan. The Moorish occupation of Spain brought the instrument to Europe, where it inspired the development of the lute and guitar. The contemporary '*ūd* is popular to the point of being iconic across the region, as guests will discern from the instrument's presence throughout MIM's Middle East and North Africa gallery.

The Morocco exhibit highlights instruments and music influenced centuries ago by customs in Spain and neighboring North African countries. Bowed and plucked lutes, drums, flutes, and the violin make up the core of Moroccan-Andalusian ensembles.

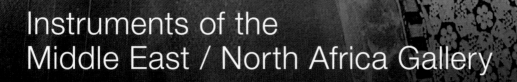

Instruments of the
Middle East / North Africa Gallery

Khatam tār from Iran (page 51)

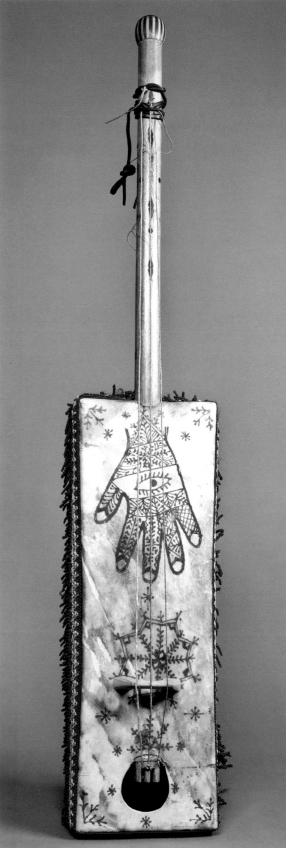

Genbri (plucked lute)

ALGERIA, MID-TO-LATE 20TH c.
Wood, goatskin, textile, gut,
mother-of-pearl
47¼ x 7¹¹⁄₁₆ x 5⅛ in.
Ex René Grémaux Collection

Genbri lutes are played
throughout North Africa by
members of the Gnawa Muslim
brotherhood. The *hamsa,* or
"hand of Fatima," design is
made with henna and is meant
to ward off the "evil eye."

Curator's Note

At the age of 15, a young Tuareg girl traditionally constructs her first *imzad* from recycled materials. She will only perform in public after several years of practice in private.

Imzad (bowed spike lute)

TUAREG PEOPLE, AHAGGAR REGION, ALGERIA, 20ᵀᴴ c.
Gourd, goatskin, wood, horsehair
25¼ x 14¼ x 8¼ in.

Also known as *anzad,* this bowed lute is the most emblematic instrument used by the Tuareg people of Saharan Africa. Most *imzad* performers are female. Men may also play it, but they must perform a different repertoire.

Tbal (double-headed cylindrical drum)

TÉTOUAN, MOROCCO, c. 1930
Lemon wood, goatskin, rope
11 x 11¼ in.

The floral and geometric patterns on this drum reflect a typically Moroccan taste for decoration. The drum may have been played as part of Arab-Andalusian ensembles and shows evidence of extensive use.

Rbab (bowed lute)

MOROCCO, MID-20TH c.
Walnut and other woods, goatskin,
cane, gut, horsehair
22½ x 8 x 7½ in.

Boat-shaped *rbab* lutes like this
are quintessentially Moroccan.
Muslims likely brought the
instrument to Morocco from the
Andalusian region of Spain.

'Ūd (plucked lute)

BAGHDAD, IRAQ, 2010
Wood, nylon
Farhan Hassan, maker
32 x 15 x 8½ in.

Hassan is a renowned *'ūd* maker in Baghdad. The leaf motif shown in the pickguard of this instrument is one of his hallmarks. The sound hole features the maker's name in a calligraphic monogram modeled after those used by the Ottoman sultans.

Khatam tonbak (goblet drum)

IRAN, 20TH c.

Mulberry and rosewood, animal skin, camel bone, brass
Parvis Amir Ataie and Golriz Khatami, makers
17½ x 11 in.
Courtesy of Golriz Khatami

This drum is the result of an unusual collaboration between master instrument maker Ataie, who made the drum from a block of mulberry wood, and *khatam* inlay artist Khatami. The masterful *khatam* marquetry is made up of thousands of individual pieces of wood, brass, and camel bone.

Curator's Note

Master *khatam* artist Golriz Khatami spent approximately 2,000 hours putting the delicate pieces for the marquetry together and applying them to the body of this drum.

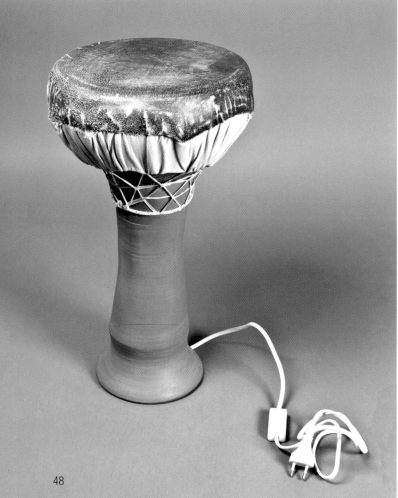

Dohola (goblet drum)

ROSH HAAYIN, ISRAEL, 2011
Clay, fishskin, lightbulb
Kobi Hagoel, maker
19 x 11½ in.

Drummers often hold their drumhead close to a fire to tighten the drumhead and improve the sound. This innovative Israeli goblet drum has a lightbulb built in to heat the head for tuning purposes.

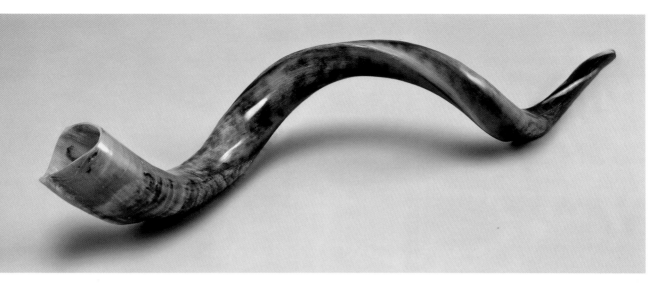

Shofar (trumpet)

ISRAEL, c. 2000
Kudu horn
37 x 7¼ x 6¼ in.

The shofar is an important symbol of Jewish heritage, being the only surviving liturgical instrument in use since ancient times. Its specific use varies throughout the many practices of Judaism, but its primary function is that of a signaling instrument.

Curator's Note

Most shofars are made from ram horns, but Yemenite Jews play longer instruments like this made from kudu horns.

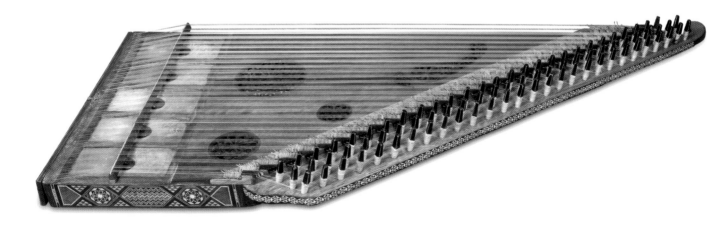

Qanun (plucked zither)

CAIRO, EGYPT, 1976
Walnut and rosewood, fishskin, metal
Gaby Tutunigy, maker
44 x 20½ x 3½ in.

Known for its bright sound and the rapid musical ornamentations of its players, the *qanun* is popular in Arab and Andalusian art-music ensembles. Tutunigy is remembered as one of the finest makers of *qanuns*.

Barbat (plucked lute)

ISFAHAN, IRAN, 2003
Spruce, rosewood, and
Persian walnut woods; metal
Masoud and Saeed Mohammadi, makers
31½ x 12 x 8¾ in.

The historical Persian *barbat* may have
been the inspiration for the development
of the *'ūd*. This modern reinterpretation
was constructed from a design by
instrument maker and researcher Ustad
Ebrahim Ghanbari.

Khatam tār (plucked lute)

IRAN, LATE 20ᵀᴴ c.
Wood, animal skin, plastic, metal
36½ x 9 x 9½ in.
*Gift in memory of Parviz Nozari by
Moe and Lois Nozari*

The distinctively shaped *tār* is
a Persian instrument that may
date back to the late 18ᵗʰ century.
The contemporary *tār* seen here
features *khatam* marquetry inlay
that is meant to reference Persian
ornamental designs.

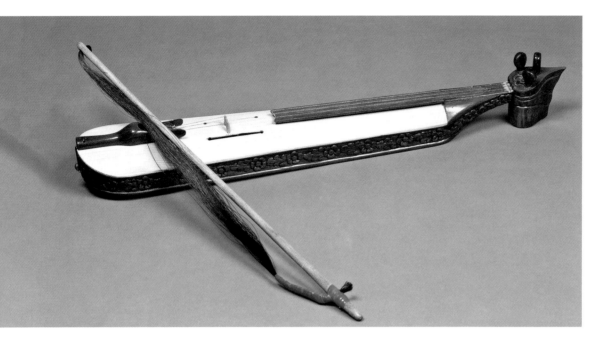

Karadeniz kemençesi (bowed lute)
BLACK SEA REGION, TURKEY, 1978
Juniper and pinewood
22½ x 4 x 2½ in.

Turkish *karadeniz kemençesi* players
often stand up and lead a folk dance
while playing. The elongated shape of this
example is characteristic of instruments
played in the Black Sea region of Turkey.

Tulum (bagpipe)
BLACK SEA REGION, TURKEY, 2000
Goatskin, boxwood, bamboo, cotton
Murat Atacan, maker
25 x 14 x 2 in.

In the Black Sea region, a *tulum* bagpipe of
this type is often played in folk ensembles
with a *kemençesi* to accompany dancing.

Did You Know?
Bagpipes likely originated in the Mediterranean
regions of Turkey or Africa. By medieval times,
they were common throughout North Africa,
the Middle East, Europe, and Asia.

Cümbüş (plucked lute)

ISTANBUL, TURKEY, 1931
Metal, wood, animal skin
Onnik Karibyan, maker
32 x 10¼ x 5½ in.

The *cümbüş* is strongly associated with the Roma people, commonly known as Gypsies. This particularly fine example was made by Onnik Karibyan, an acclaimed Armenian luthier who established his shop in Istanbul. Karibyan remained active until his death in 1976, and his *'ūds* and other string instruments are very highly regarded.

Zorna (double-reed pipe)

KURDISH PEOPLE, TURKEY, c. 1950
Wood, metal, stones
12 x 3¼ in.

Kurdish people play the blaring double-reed *zorna* together with a large bass drum to accompany their signature circular dances. This example features classic metal ornamentation adorned with semiprecious stones.

The Egypt exhibit showcases instruments played in the distinctive musical style that emerged in Cairo during the late 20th century. These urban performances melded time-honored traditions with innovation.

The Iraq exhibit highlights instruments like the bowed *jōza* and the goblet-shaped *khishba* drum. Master artisans continue to construct instruments in Iraq, despite political turmoil.

(right) **The Iran exhibit** displays instruments from the country's diverse ethnic groups alongside classical Persian instruments.

IRAN

Middle East / North Africa

Exhibit made possible through the generosity of
Moe and Lois Nozari
in memory of Parviz Nozari

Kamāncheh (bowed spike lute)
Lors people; Khorram-abad, Lorestan
Province, 2009
Mulberry and walnut woods, animal skin,
metal, horsehair
Mohammadi, maker
Displayed with bow

Robab (plucked lute)
Tehran, 2009
Mulberry and walnut woods
Mani Jahisfi, maker

19th-century gong from Brunei (page 74)

Asia Gallery

ASIA

The largest continent on earth, Asia is surrounded by the Pacific, Arctic, and Indian Oceans. The Asia gallery at MIM is home to over 1,200 objects that illustrate the cultural and musical variety of this expansive region.

Asia is the world's most diverse continent. Its geography ranges from snowy mountains to tropical islands, from dense cities to quiet villages. Its peoples, too, are among the world's most varied—from the Han in China to the diminishing minority groups of India and Southeast Asia. And Asia's music is just as varied, reflecting myriad languages and ways of life.

Asian musical traditions have been shaped over centuries, as people traveled by land and sea along trade routes spanning vast territories. Merchants and travelers exchanged silk and spices as well as ideas, languages, music, and musical instruments. Historical evidence reveals that music traveled in every direction, and by the eleventh century musical instruments from the Middle East and Central Asia could be found both in Europe and in parts of East, South, and Southeast Asia.

The Boat Lutes exhibit showcases a popular instrument that is distinctive to the islands of Southeast Asia. Named for their boat-like shape, these lutes are carved from a single block of wood, and are often adorned with representations of animals.

In MIM's Asia gallery, guests learn about characteristic instruments and ensembles of Southeast Asia, East Asia, South Asia, and from Central Asia and the Caucasus.

The Asia gallery at MIM is organized by geographical region, displaying characteristic instruments and musical ensembles from Southeast Asia, East Asia, South Asia, and from Central Asia and the Caucasus.

The Southeast Asia subgallery displays diverse wind, percussion, and string instruments, including a stunning collection of "boat lutes"—plucked lutes and zithers from an area of maritime Southeast Asia where the Philippines, Malaysia, Brunei, and Indonesia meet. In many Southeast Asian countries musicians play gongs and gong-chime ensembles. They use flat, knobbed, and decorated single gongs and also construct ensembles with gongs arranged

as melody instruments. This is the case in Javanese and Balinese gamelan orchestras and in similar ensembles in other parts of Indonesia, as well as in Malaysia, the Philippines, Cambodia, and Burma (Myanmar).

The instruments of East Asia show musical intersections influenced by travel and trade among the peoples of China, Taiwan, Mongolia, Japan, and South and North Korea. An ancient Chinese classification system organized instruments by the materials of which they were made. Instruments that exemplify this system— such as stone chimes, metal bells, long zithers, pear-shaped lutes, and decorated drums—appear in varying forms in MIM's displays for several countries. Guests can

The Gamelan exhibit at MIM showcases a majestic Javanese gamelan as it might be played for a performance of traditional *wayang kulit,* Indonesia's popular shadow puppetry.

also see instruments linked to religious traditions of Tibet, including drums, double-reed woodwinds, and long horns of different sizes. In the Taiwan exhibit, indigenous jaw harps and nose flutes reveal relationships to Southeast Asia and the Pacific Islands, while the instruments and musical practices of Mongolia reflect its people's nomadic lives.

MIM's South Asia collection features music from the diverse regions of India, Afghanistan, Nepal, Bhutan, Pakistan, Bangladesh, Sri Lanka, and the Maldives. The music of India offers a great variety of instruments and musical styles, including classical ensembles pairing finely decorated lutes with accompanying

drums, and regional instrumental practices associated with local musical events. Other South Asia exhibits show relationships among all the countries, and feature double-headed drums, finely carved lutes, curved horns, masks, and brightly colored dance clothing.

In Central Asia and the Caucasus, musical instruments of Kazakhstan, Kyrgyzstan, Uzbekistan, Tajikistan, Turkmenistan, Azerbaijan, Armenia, and Georgia show how their musics relate to Asia, the Middle East, and Europe. The finely made plucked and bowed lutes, especially, show how master instrument makers have kept their art alive by passing down their skills from generation to generation.

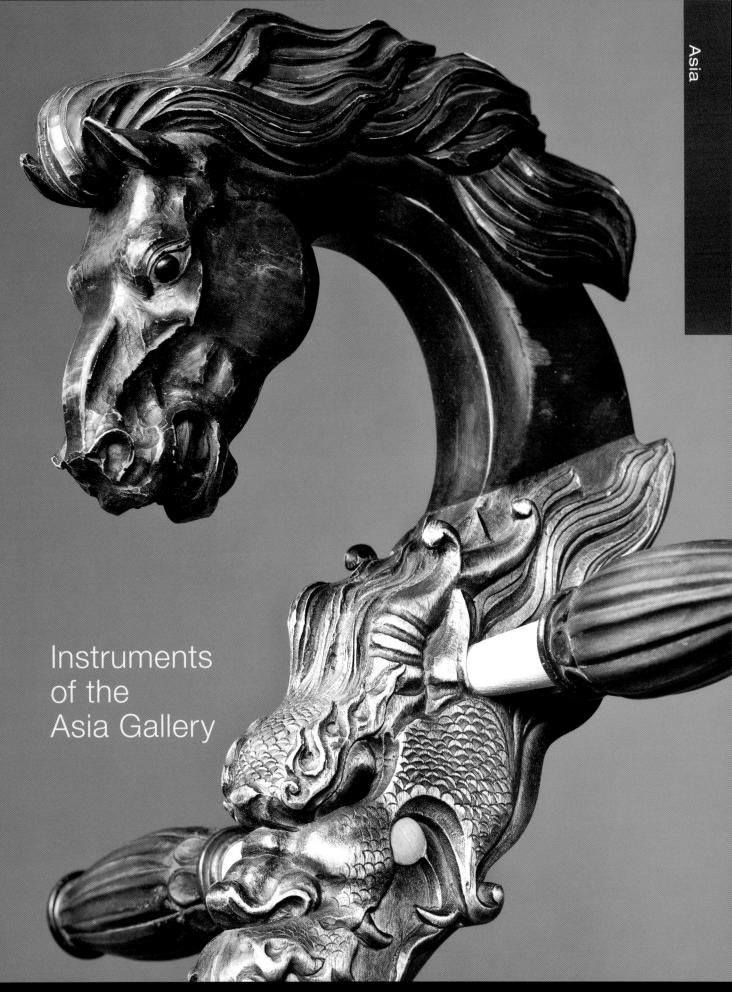

Instruments
of the
Asia Gallery

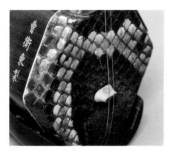

Erhu (bowed spike lute)

BEIJING, CHINA, 2009
Wood, python skin, horsehair
Cao Weidong, maker
32 x 4 x 6¼ in.

Bowed lutes like the *erhu* entered China from Central Asia, becoming essential to the sound of Chinese musical traditions such as opera and *sizhu*. This *erhu* was made for MIM by a master instrument maker in Beijing.

Tonggu (gong)

BUYI PEOPLE, GUIZHOU PROVINCE, CHINA, 1940–1950
Bronze
12 x 20¼ in.

The tradition of making and playing *tonggu* probably originated in Southeast Asia. The Chinese name translates to "bronze drum." Instruments of this type are still made and played among some indigenous groups in China, Laos, Vietnam, Thailand, and Burma. This example features the animals of the Chinese zodiac around the central sun pattern.

Curator's Note

Gongs like the *tonggu* have been found in archaeological excavations all over Asia, some dating back to 400 BC in China and Southeast Asia.

Paigu (hourglass drum)
YANGSHAO PEOPLE, XI'AN PROVINCE, CHINA, LATE 5TH–MID-4TH MILLENNIUM BC
Ceramic
6½ x 4¾ in.
Gift of Henry C.C. LU

Found near Banpo village in Xi'an Province, this drum dates back to China's Neolithic period, some 4,000 to 7,000 years ago. The drumhead, possibly frog or snakeskin, would have been tied to the hooks around the rim of the drum for tension. Yangshao people may have played drums of this type for rituals or religious ceremonies.

Curator's Note
The *paigu* is the oldest instrument in MIM's collection.

O (scraper)
PAJU, GYEONGGI PROVINCE, SOUTH KOREA, 2009
Wood, bamboo
Kim Hyun-gon, maker
36 x 16 x 15½ in.

The *o* was used for Confucian ritual music in Korean imperial court. The wooden tiger's notched back is scraped with a piece of split bamboo to indicate the beginning and end of each musical piece.

Biwa (plucked lute)

TENRI, NARA, JAPAN, 2007–2008
Paulownia wood, silk
Tanakaya, maker
43 x 16½ x 9 in.

The *biwa* is related to the Chinese *pipa,* which is based on Persian instruments similar to the Arabic *'ūd* and on the European lute.

Huxtar (bowed lute)

UYGHUR PEOPLE, KASHGAR, XINJIANG, CHINA, 2006
Apricot and chenar woods, plastic inlay
Mehmet Imin Qadi, maker
28 x 8½ x 7¾ in.

The Uyghur people of Northwest China trace their roots to Central Asia. This relationship is manifested in the *'ūd*-like shape of this bowed lute, as well as the elaborate geometric patterned inlay typical of their instruments.

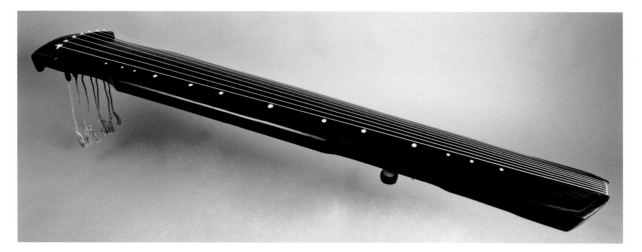

Qin (plucked zither)

CHINA, 1888
Wood, silk
47 x 8 x 3 in.

Early examples of the Chinese *qin* date back to the 2nd century BC. The zither's construction reflects the three most important factors in the traditional Chinese view of the universe. The convex shape of the playing surface symbolizes heaven, the flat underside signifies earth, and the player represents man. The inscription on the underside of the instrument reads "Jade Pendant" (a poetic name for this particular *qin*) and gives the date of construction and possibly the maker's name.

Yangqin (struck zither)

BEIJING, CHINA, 2009
Wood, metal, mother-of-pearl
Fan Ruwu, maker
46¼ x 20¾ x 6 in.

The *yangqin* is adapted from the Persian *santur.* In the 20th century, Chinese makers enlarged the zither and extended its pitch range to over three octaves. The modern *yangqin* is an important part of *sizhu* (silk-and-bamboo) ensembles.

Taiko (double-headed barrel drum)

TENRI, NARA PREFECTURE, JAPAN, 2007–2008
Wood, animal skin, metal, silk
8¾ x 21¾ in.

Taiko is the Japanese word for "drum." An important instrument in the stately *gagaku* performance, the *taiko* marks the main beat for each musical phrase. This *taiko* is decorated with lions, which are traditional symbols of strength and protection.

Gakuso (plucked zither)

JAPAN, LATE 19TH c.
Paulownia wood, silk
76 x 11 x 6½ in.

The *gakuso* is intended for use in *gagaku*—the ritual music of imperial courts. With 13 silk strings, the *gakuso* typically plays repeating musical patterns as part of *gagaku* string and wind repertoire.

Did You Know?

The *gakuso* is similar to another Japanese zither, the more common *koto*.

Shakuhachi (notched flute)

JAPAN, 20ᵀᴴ c.
Madaké bamboo
22 x 2 in.

Formerly associated with monks of the Fuke sect of Zen Buddhism, this bamboo flute and its distinctive breathy sound are important components of *sankyoku* music. The *shakuhachi* is meticulously crafted from the root end of *madaké* bamboo.

Curator's Note

The name *shakuhachi* is derived from an obsolete system of measurement describing the flute's traditional length.

Ever büree (single-reed pipe)

MONGOL PEOPLE, ULAANBAATAR, MONGOLIA, 2008
Wood, cow horn, brass, cane
Atumbatar, maker
17½ x 13½ x 4½ in.

Developed in Ulaanbaatar over 30 years ago, the *ever büree* combines the Mongolian *büree* long trumpet, the simple animal horn, and the European clarinet or saxophone.

Sheng (mouth organ)

CHINA, 20TH c.
Bamboo, metal
20 x 8 x 4¼ in.
Gift of Frank and Marilyn Beddor

The origin of this ancient Chinese instrument is believed to predate 600 BC. The *sheng* is played by covering finger holes and blowing into a wind chamber where hidden free reeds vibrate to produce sound. This chamber, at the base of the instrument, was once constructed of gourd or wood but is now typically made of metal.

Did You Know?
The bamboo pipes of a *sheng* are traditionally arranged to resemble the wings of a mythical *fenghuang,* or phoenix.

Sanshin (plucked spike lute)

OKINAWAN PEOPLE, OKINAWA, JAPAN, LATE 20TH c.
Wood, python skin, textile, ivory
31 x 8¾ x 3¾ in.
Gift of Robert Garfias

Popular for accompanying folk songs, the *sanshin* has become an iconic symbol of Okinawan music and identity. The player uses a large plectrum, or pick, carved from water buffalo horn or ivory. The instrument's python-skin resonator and relatively short neck set it apart from its longer-necked cousin, the Japanese *shamisen.*

Morin khuur
(bowed spike lute)

**MONGOL PEOPLE,
MONGOLIA, 2009**
Birch, spruce, and
ebony woods; horsehair
*Bayarsaikhan Badamsuren,
maker*
43¼ x 12 x 7½ in.

This beautifully carved
morin khuur, made
for MIM by a master
instrument maker,
contains fine carvings
of the horse so beloved
in Mongolia, as well as
representations of four
animals highly regarded
in Buddhist tradition:
the tiger and lion, and a
mythical bird *(khangarid)*
and dragon.

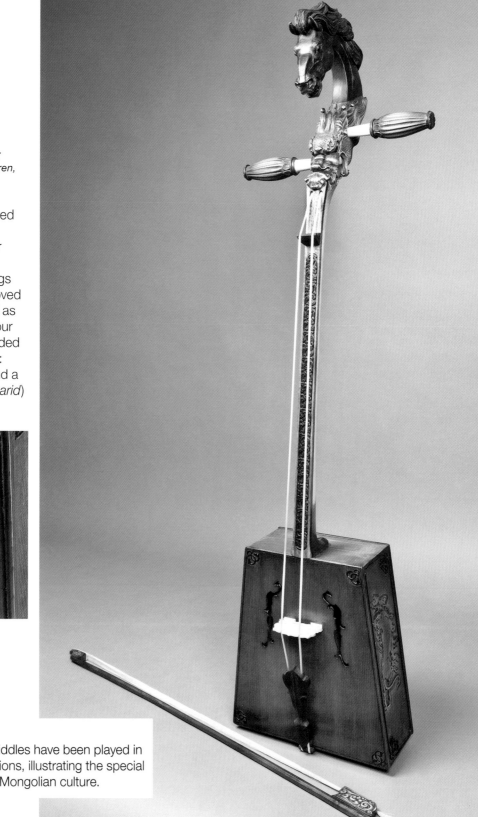

Curator's Note
Bowed horse-head fiddles have been played in
Mongolia for generations, illustrating the special
place horses hold in Mongolian culture.

Kamaicā (bowed lute)

RAJASTHAN, INDIA, 20ᵀᴴ c.
Wood, animal skin, ivory, mother-of-pearl
29 x 12¾ x 7½ in.

This bowed lute is played by Manganihār performers in Rajasthan to accompany singing. These Muslim musicians are known for playing Hindu devotional music for wealthy patrons in Hindu temples. The *kamaicā* is slowly being replaced by the harmonium among younger Manganihār musicians.

Pungī (reed pipe)

MANGANIHĀR PEOPLE, RAJASTHAN, INDIA, 20ᵀᴴ c.
Gourd, bamboo, metal, textile, beads
23½ x 4½ x 4 in.
Ex Gérard Coppéré Collection

This wind instrument is widely used in many parts of India by itinerant musicians and other entertainers, including snake charmers. Experts suggest that the snakes may actually respond to the player's movements rather than the instrument's sound. The bright colors and ornaments on this example help draw the audience's attention to the performer.

Tambūrī (plucked lute)

KARNATAKA, INDIA, c. 1890
Wood, animal bone
35¹³⁄₁₆ x 9¹³⁄₁₆ x 5⅞ in.

This painted *tambūrī* features figures of musicians depicted in the style of Indian miniature painting once popular in the Muslim and Hindu courts.

Tānpūrā (plucked lute)

KOLKATA, INDIA, 2009
Tun and red cedarwood,
gourd, plastic inlay
*Sanat Halder, Somjit Dasgupta,
and Mohan Lal Sharma, makers*
53 x 16 x 9½ in.

Traditionally constructed from a
flat gourd, this beautifully inlaid
plucked lute is made in a style
known as *kachuā* (tortoise),
because the *tumba* (sound box)
looks like the back of a tortoise.

Vichitra vina (plucked lute)

LAHORE, PAKISTAN, 1960–1969
Wood, gourd, animal bone
53⁹⁄₁₆ x 13 x 21⅞ in.

Players of this rare Hindustani instrument change and bend notes by
moving a glass or metal slide along the length of the strings, much like
a slide guitar. The bird at the end of the body is a peacock.

Jakhē (plucked zither)

THAILAND, 2008
Jackfruit and gardenia woods, nylon
Nattapan Champarlee, maker
53¾ x 18½ x 11½ in.

This finely made, inlaid zither is used in Thai *mahori* ensembles. The name *jakhē* is derived from the Thai word *jarakhe,* meaning "crocodile." Earlier examples looked more like crocodiles, but current instruments bear only a vague resemblance to the animal.

Tawak tawak (gong)

MALAY PEOPLE, BRUNEI, c. 1850
Bronze
4¾ x 19½ in.

This gong was made using a special process called "lost wax," or *cire perdue,* which enables the fine relief adorning these highly regarded instruments.

Đàn bầu (plucked zither)

VIỆT PEOPLE, HO CHI MINH CITY (FORMERLY SAIGON), VIETNAM, 1992
Burmese rosewood and Chinese parasol wood, buffalo-horn, mother-of-pearl, steel
Bá Phước, maker
40¾ x 6½ x 15¾ in.

This one-stringed box zither uses a flexible buffalo-horn "neck" to bend the harmonics of a plucked note. It was once common as a beggar's instrument, but is also associated with scholars and the Trần imperial court (1225–1400). Today, musicians continue to use the *đàn bầu* to accompany singing, or, with the use of amplification, as a melodic instrument in classical ensembles.

Hegelung (plucked lute)

T'BOLI PEOPLE, SOUTH COTABATO, PHILIPPINES, c. 2000
Wood, beeswax, horsehair, metal
52 x 7¼ x 5 in.
Ex Hans Brandeis Collection

The *hegelung* (or *hagelung*) is played by T'boli men and women. Carved from a single block of wood, these "boat lutes" are distinctive instruments found in island regions of Southeast Asia.

Kuglung (plucked lute)

MATIGSALUG MANOBO PEOPLE, DAVAO CITY, PHILIPPINES, c. 1997
Wood, beeswax, bamboo
Camilo Gulam, maker
62 x 7¼ x 7 in.
Ex Hans Brandeis Collection

The maker of this "boat lute" is also a respected performer. He used this instrument to show his skills at instrument making and carpentry. The peghead is carved to resemble a horse, and the pattern of dots and lines is burnt into the wood with a heated nail. The bright reddish finish is unusual for Manobo instruments.

The Cambodia exhibit showcases a wide variety of Khmer performing arts, from stately *mohori* and *pinn peat* ensembles to folk instruments from rural villages. Masks and puppets highlight Cambodia's thriving dance-drama and its endangered shadow puppetry.

The Mongolia exhibit features instruments and objects that illustrate Mongolians' relationship with the places and animals around them. The large *tsam* costume points out a revival of Buddhist traditions in post-communist Mongolia.

(right) **The Sri Lanka exhibit** focuses on the driving rhythms of Sinhalese *kolam* dance-drama with a drummer's fanciful costume. Masks worn by dancers illustrate the battle between a bird-man from Hindu mythology and powerful cobras. *(Mannequin design by Créations Isabelle de Borchgrave)*

Mud drum from Papua New Guinea (page 85)

Oceania Gallery

OCEANIA

American Samoa
Australia
Cook Islands
Easter Island
Fiji
French Polynesia
Guam (U.S. territory)
Hawaii
Indonesia
Kiribati
Marshall Islands
Micronesia, Federated States of
Nauru
New Caledonia
New Zealand
Niue
Norfolk Island
Palau
Papua New Guinea
Pitcairn Islands
Samoa
Solomon Islands
Tokelau
Tonga
Tuvalu
Vanuatu

Oceania includes thousands of tropical islands in the Pacific Ocean. It contains Australia, the only country on earth that covers an entire continent, and also the U.S. Hawaiian Islands. MIM's Oceania gallery presents the images, artifacts, and instruments that are part of this region's rich musical traditions.

MIM's Oceania gallery represents the many island nations that make up Melanesia, Micronesia, and Polynesia, as well as Australia and New Zealand. Oceania includes more than twenty thousand islands, from the vast continent of Australia to the tiny islands scattered across the Pacific Ocean. The bulk of the region's thirty million people inhabit only about fifteen hundred of these islands. The indigenous peoples of Oceania share a close connection to the arts; their musical traditions demonstrate an especially strong relationship between music and dance.

SOLOMON ISLANDS

The Solomon Islands exhibit includes giant bamboo instruments that resemble smaller panpipes. The player does not blow into these large instruments but, rather, slaps the tube openings with the sole of a sandal.

MIM's Oceania gallery presents a stunning variety of sights and sounds from diverse peoples and nations.

The Melanesia region is home to a remarkable diversity of peoples, languages, and musical instruments. The many peoples of Papua New Guinea and eastern Indonesia are known for fancifully carved flutes and slit drums as well as distinctive handheld hourglass drums that accompany dances and songs. Vanuatu is well known for the extensive use of slit drums, some of which measure nearly nineteen feet in length and are among the largest musical instruments in the world.

In Micronesia, and to a lesser extent in Polynesia, hand clapping and body percussion accompany song and dance performances. MIM's collection from these regions also includes slit drums, flutes, ukuleles, and large shell trumpets. Although the work of nineteenth-century colonial administrators discouraged some indigenous musical practices, contemporary interisland music festivals and competitions give younger generations a forum from which to learn and build upon fundamental Polynesian traditions.

The Australia collection highlights traditional arts and musical-instrument making among the Aboriginal peoples. Of particular interest is the painted *yidaki.* Commonly known as a *didjeridu,* the instrument originated in Australia's northwestern region and spread to other parts of the country relatively recently. The New Zealand exhibit features instruments inspired by modern research on traditional instruments and practices, some of which had all but disappeared. European music imported by colonists from the British Isles continues to flourish in the region, giving rise to makers of fine guitars and folk instruments. Innovative makers have also drawn upon the influence of more recent immigrants from Asia to create completely new instruments.

From monumental slit drums to tiny flutes, MIM's Oceania gallery presents a stunning variety of sights and sounds from diverse peoples and nations. The instruments and exhibits in this gallery will completely immerse guests in the dynamic musical world of the Pacific.

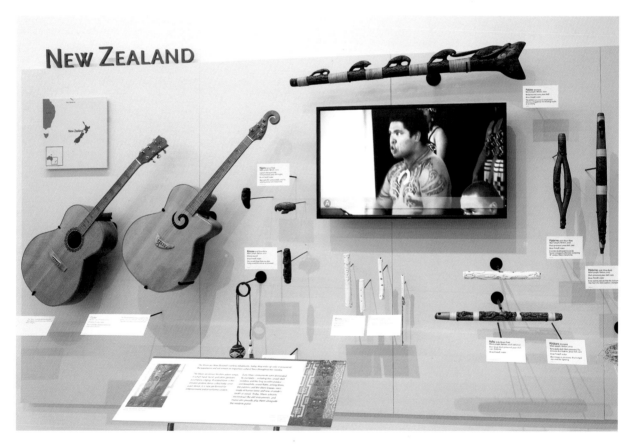

The New Zealand exhibit highlights instruments from the country's earliest people, the Maori, who primarily crafted trumpets and flutes. Today's musicians may play traditional instruments together with the modern guitar.

Instruments of the
Oceania Gallery

Kundu
(single-headed hourglass drum)

**TAMI ISLANDS, MOROBE PROVINCE,
PAPUA NEW GUINEA, MID-20TH c.**
Wood, monitor lizard skin
6½ x 29 in.

Four ancestral faces decorate the top and
bottom sections of this beautifully carved
drum. Snakes decorate the body and
handle along one side. Hourglass-shaped
kundu drums are ubiquitous throughout
New Guinea.

Garamut (slit drum)

**IATMUL PEOPLE, MARAMBA VILLAGE, MIDDLE SEPIK,
EAST SEPIK PROVINCE, PAPUA NEW GUINEA, 2008**
Wood, cowry shells
Plasios Asapi, maker
119 x 21 x 29 in.

Made by hollowing out a tree trunk through a four- to five-inch-wide slit, the *garamut* is used to communicate messages, call people together, and accompany dance and song. The carvings on each end represent animal spirits important to the Iatmul people; the bas-relief on the sides illustrates everyday village life. Asapi (1945–2009) learned the art of carving from his grandfather.

Mud drum

**KOROGO VILLAGE, MIDDLE SEPIK,
PAPUA NEW GUINEA, 1970s**
Wood
6½ x 22 x 18 in.

This instrument is agitated on an area of mud, and the resulting suction produces a variety of sounds. This mud drum was played during an initiation ceremony in Korogo Village, where it was collected. Mud plays an important role in the mythologies of many New Guinean peoples.

Side-blown trumpet

KANDUANAM, EAST SEPIK PROVINCE, PAPUA NEW GUINEA, 20TH C.
Wood
38 x 9 in.

Many peoples of the Sepik River basin once used trumpets like this to herald a head-hunting raid and to announce its successful completion. This instrument is carved with numerous faces, snakes, crocodiles, and decorative patterns that relate to the environment and local beliefs.

Imunu viki
(bullroarer)

GULF PROVINCE, PAPUA NEW GUINEA, 19TH C. AND 20TH C.
Wood
16½ x 2¾ in.; 18 x 2¼ in.

Tied to a string and whirled over the player's head, these instruments make an unearthly sound. Many peoples of Papua New Guinea equate the bullroarer sound with voices of the spirit world. People in the Gulf Province often made these instruments to resemble large masks used in ceremonial dances.

Atingting (slit drum)

FANLA VILLAGE, NORTH AMBRYN, VANUATU, 2005
Breadfruit wood
Freddy Bule, maker
102 x 13 x 17½ in.

Noted for their artistry, enormous vertical slit drums such as this are unique to the central parts of Vanuatu. Carved from an entire tree trunk, the drum can be as tall as 19 feet. When hit with a stick, the hollowed cavity functions as a large resonating chamber that projects sound for miles.

Debusech (shell trumpet)

PALAU, 19TH c.
Triton shell
13 x 7 x 5¼ in.

Shell trumpets like this one are used by Palauans to play various musical messages. They may announce the beginning of a celebration or inform the community of a chief's death.

Curator's Note

Traditionally, groups of drums were "planted" in a village dancing ground to provide complex rhythmic accompaniment for dances. They were also used to communicate from village to village.

Tariparau
(double-headed cylindrical drum)

**PAPEETE, TAHITI,
FRENCH POLYNESIA, 2008–2010**
Hibiscus wood, goatskin, rope
19½ x 22½ in.

Tōʻere (slit drum and beater)

**PAPEETE, TAHITI,
FRENCH POLYNESIA, 1996**
Pacific rosewood
Tom Urima, maker
31⅝ x 7¹¹⁄₁₆ in.

Mixed percussion groups are common in Tahiti. The *tariparau* drum plays a basic pulse that accompanies the interlocking lead patterns of the *tōʻere*. This *tōʻere* was not only made by a respected carver, but from 1996 until 2010 it was played by some of the most highly regarded Tahitian performers.

Soprano ukulele (plucked lute)

HONOLULU, HAWAII, USA, 1915–1925
Koa wood, metal, nylon
Jonah Kumalae, maker
21¼ x 6¼ x 3¼ in.

Portuguese immigrants began making ukuleles in Hawaii in the 1880s. By the early 1910s, native Hawaiians were also making these instruments; Jonah Kumalae (1895–1940) was one of the first significant manufacturers. The beautifully grained koa wood and fine appointments on this Kumalae ukulele reveal that it is a premium model.

'Ulī'ulī (rattle)

KANEOHE, OAHU, HAWAII, USA, 1965
Gourd, pebbles, chicken feathers, mulberry bark
Kau'i Zuttermeister, maker
9¼ x 14¼ in.; 8¼ x 11½ in.

Hula performers can hold one or two *'ulī'ulī* rattles, shaking and striking them against their bodies as part of the dance movements.

Did You Know?

Legendary English explorer Captain James Cook and his maritime crew are said to have witnessed a *hula 'ulī'ulī* dance during their expedition to Hawaii in 1779.

Bark painting and
Yidaki (natural trumpet)

YOLNGU PEOPLE, NORTH CENTRAL ARNHEM LAND, NORTHERN TERRITORY, AUSTRALIA, 1960–1969

Eucalyptus bark; eucalyptus wood
Mick Magani (Mildjingi clan), maker and artist
28 7/8 x 13 3/4 x 2 3/4 in. (painting)
59 x 2 3/4 in. (*yidaki*)

Magani, a renowned Aboriginal artist and instrument maker, became a ceremonial leader in his community. This matching *yidaki* and painting include intricate animal and plant motifs in natural pigments. The *yidaki*, also called *"didjeridu"* by Europeans, is played in rituals and to accompany secular dance.

Did You Know?
British broadcaster and naturalist David Attenborough describes artist Mick Magani in detail in his 1963 book, *Quest under Capricorn*.

"Blue Mountain" guitar

BOTANY, NEW SOUTH WALES, AUSTRALIA, 2009
Tasmanian blackwood, Queensland maple, and Engelmann
spruce woods; mother-of-pearl; *paua* shell
Gilet Guitars, maker
41 x 15½ x 4½ in.

Commissioned for MIM, this guitar is made
predominantly from Australian woods and other
natural materials. Expert luthiers Gerard Gilet,
Darrell Wheeler, Michael Penberthy, and Beau
Hannam of Gilet Guitars collaborated to build the
guitar and have all signed the interior label. The
kingfisher inlay on the headstock is made from
local mother-of-pearl and *paua* shell.

Tarhu (plucked and bowed lute)

ARMIDALE, NEW SOUTH WALES, AUSTRALIA, 2009
Boxwood, blackwood, and ebony; metal
Peter Biffen, maker
48 x 11 x 9¾ in.

This innovative Australian-made instrument combines elements of various Asian spike lutes such as the Chinese *erhu*, the Turkish *tanbur,* and the Azeri *kamancha*. The four melody strings can be played with a bow or plucked, and eight sympathetic strings add to the sound. The round body of the instrument conceals a wooden cone resonator of Biffen's own design.

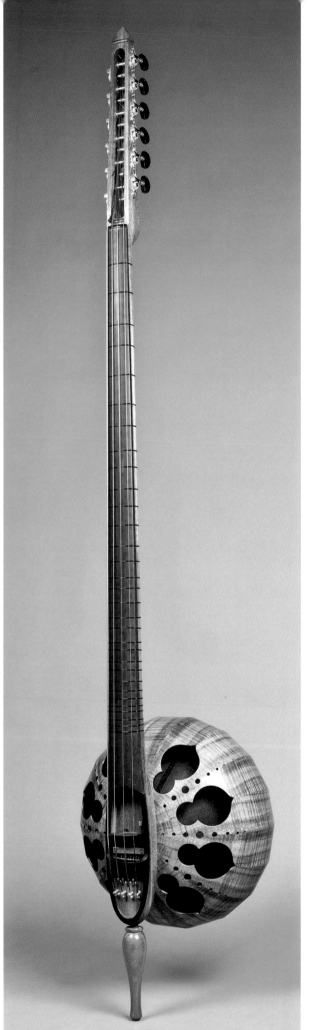

Pūkāea (trumpet)

NELSON, NEW ZEALAND, 2007
Red pinewood, cane, *paua* shell
Brian Flintoff, maker
45 x 7¼ x 4⅜ in.

Once used by the Maori as a signaling trumpet, the *pūkāea* was also utilized as a megaphone for shouting insults at enemies. This example was inspired by New Zealand author Margaret Orbell's book, *Birds of Aotearoa*; it features figures of several local birds, including the extinct giant moa, whose voice the author likens to the sound of a *pūkāea*.

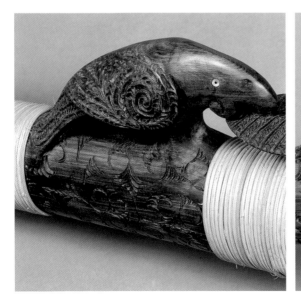

Pūtōrino
(double end-blown flute)

NELSON, NEW ZEALAND, 2007
Black pinewood, *paua* shell, cane
Brian Flintoff, maker
16½ x 3¼ x 2 in.

Only a few original examples of
the double *pūtōrino* exist today,
and the exact techniques that
were once used to play it remain a
mystery. Researchers theorize that
the instrument can be played both
as a flute and as a "bugle." This
example was inspired by historic
Maori instruments in museum
collections and descriptions from
early travel documents.

"Miromiro" guitar

KERIKERI, BAY OF ISLANDS, NEW ZEALAND, 2009
New Zealand kauri and teakwood, *paua* shell, metal
Christian Druery, maker
42 x 16 x 4½ in.

The kauri used for the guitar's back and sides was preserved underground in peat for about 50,000 years before it was salvaged for timber. The spiral headstock, sound holes, and *paua* inlay all reflect a Maori design representing an unfurling fern frond, a reminder of the way in which life changes, yet ultimately stays the same.

The West Papua exhibit includes hourglass drums, trumpets, and a full-body fiber mask from the Asmat people of western New Guinea. The peoples of the island of New Guinea share many musical practices even though they are divided politically between two countries: Indonesian West Papua and Papua New Guinea.

The Aboriginal Australia exhibit emphasizes instruments created as expressions of Aboriginal identity and culture, such as the bullroarer and the *yidaki*.

(right) **The Cook Islands exhibit** features drums that are associated with contemporary drum-dance groups and popular Pacific island festivals.

COOK ISLANDS

Dance paddle
Dance spear

Cook Islands

Dance skirt
Waist band

Kaara

Tōkere

B New Zealand

Latin America
Gallery

LATIN AMERICA

Antigua and Barbuda
Argentina
Aruba
Bahamas
Barbados
Belize
Bolivia
Bonaire
Brazil
Chile
Colombia
Costa Rica
Cuba
Curaçao
Dominica
Dominican Republic
Ecuador
El Salvador
French Guiana
Grenada
Guadeloupe
Guatemala
Guyana
Haiti
Honduras
Jamaica
Martinique
Mexico
Nicaragua
Panama
Paraguay
Peru
Puerto Rico
St. Kitts and Nevis
St. Lucia
St. Vincent and the Grenadines
Suriname
Trinidad and Tobago
Uruguay
Venezuela

From Mexico and the Caribbean islands stretching southward to the furthest tip of Argentina, Latin America is a region with impressive musical vitality. At MIM, it is presented in 38 multimedia exhibits featuring more than 500 instruments.

Latin American and Caribbean countries are characterized by youthfulness, innovation, and a blending of Old and New World cultural influences. Relative to Africa, Asia, Europe, and the Middle East, the music and most instruments characteristic of Latin America today emerged within the past five hundred years, as colonial influences from Europe and Africa merged with indigenous forms. Moreover, it was only after independent Latin American countries were formed within the last two centuries that the music from this region truly came of age.

Latin America's music has been shaped by a continuous flow of migrants into and out of the region. Today, nearly 25 percent of the U.S. population claims Latin American roots, and the Latin American presence in Europe and elsewhere

The Dominican Republic exhibit illustrates how Dominican music blends African, European, and indigenous influences, from the *marímbula* to the button accordion, from maracas to *güiras*.

is growing. But Latin American music has traveled even more than its people. Jamaican reggae, Brazilian samba, Dominican merengue, Cuban rumba, and transnational salsa music are performed and danced to in Europe, Asia, Africa, and the United States and are being transformed in the process as each new population embraces them.

In MIM's Latin America gallery, guests discover a juxtaposition of instruments with different ethnic origins and qualities of sound. Some represent the remarkable preservation of music from the Old World; others are highly original. Aiding the evolution of this Latin American mix is the existence of parallel instrument

types among indigenous, African, and European peoples, as well as the ease with which instruments travel from one musical culture to another. A wealth of frame drums, long and short cylinder drums, friction drums, musical bows, scrapers, and shakers recall direct links to precolonial African and indigenous cultures, as well as to the Iberian Peninsula. Guitars, lutes, and harps affirming Spanish, Portuguese, Arabic, and North African roots are embraced all across Latin America, while indigenous Americans and Afro-descendants have modified playing techniques and construction of these Old World instrumental models.

Instruments also flow easily from one culture to another because objects do not bond to a culture as strongly as languages or musical styles do. For example, the Guatemalan *marimba de tecomates* is modeled from an instrument introduced by central African slaves over four centuries ago. Since then, indigenous and mestizo groups have enthusiastically adopted marimbas into their own music, and in Guatemala they ceased to be associated with Afro-descendant people altogether. An invention of the mestizo culture of the Andes Mountains, the *charango* is modeled after a type of small Spanish guitar but made from the shell of an armadillo, tuned to a scale unfamiliar to European music, and strummed primarily as percussive and melodic accompaniment rather than harmonic.

In other cases, European-derived music was adopted by indigenous and Afro-descendant peoples but transformed by the invention of instruments inspired by existing traditions and local resources. In colonial Jesuit missions, indigenous musicians designed huge multiple-tube trumpets (*bajones*) to perform music in church. The ingenious steel-pan ensembles from Trinidad are used not only for playing Afro-Caribbean music but also in masterful arrangements of classical repertoire for orchestra from composers including Gershwin, Tchaikovsky, and Wagner.

The Latin America gallery illustrates how new musical cultures are created by combining elements of old ones in fresh ways. Like combining ingredients in skillful cooking, Latin American music preserves the distinct flavor of each instrument and performer. At the same time, it blends them to create a mixture that is both original and familiar, resonating with the evolving musical culture and with the dramas and rituals of Latin Americans' wider lives.

The Honduras exhibit exemplifies the concepts of ethnic blending and broad diffusion of Old World instrument models so characteristic of Latin America.

Instruments
of the
Latin America
Gallery

Rafted, multiple trumpet *(bajón)* from Buenos Aires, Argentina (page 109)

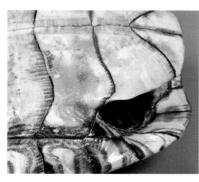

Carapacho (percussion vessel and beaters)

ZAPOTEC PEOPLE, MEXICO, 20TH c.
Tortoise shell, deer antlers
4½ x 9 x 11 in.
Ex Guillermo Contreras Arias Collection

A tortoise shell struck on the underside by deer antlers, this instrument is similar to those used by pre-Columbian cultures. Originally, several tortoise shells were played in ensembles alongside cane flutes and conch trumpets.

Rattle

MOCHE PEOPLE, NORTHERN COASTAL PERU, AD 1–200
Copper
7½ x 4 x 1¼ in.

The hollow circles around the bottom edge of this pre-Columbian copper ornament contain pebbles. It was hung alongside others, creating metal-on-metal and rattling sounds when worn as back belt flaps. The central figure represents Ai-apaec, a Moche deity associated with ritual sacrifice.

Tlalpanhuehuetl

(single-headed cylindrical drum)

MEXICO, 20TH c.
Wood, cowhide
40 x 33 in.
Ex Guillermo Contreras Arias Collection

Modeled upon elaborately carved pre-Columbian drums used in religious ceremonies and dances, this instrument is used in contemporary reconstructions of Aztec traditions.

Curator's Note

Because the sound of the large Aztec-style drums resonates across great distances, in some villages in the valleys of central Mexico they are still played to announce the opening of patron-saint festivals and other major Christian ceremonies.

Tahuitol
(musical bow with gourd resonator)

**MEXICANERO PEOPLE,
STATE OF DURANGO, MEXICO, 20TH c.**
Wood, gourd, cord
39⅜ x 1¾ x 3¾ in. (bow)
7⅝ x 13⅛ in. (gourd)
Ex Guillermo Contreras Arias Collection

Musical bows are common in both Africa
and indigenous America. With some
bows, the musician's mouth is used as
a resonator, but like the Afro-Brazilian
berimbau, this indigenous bow comes
with a gourd resonator.

Sacabuche (friction drum)

OCOTEPEQUE, HONDURAS, 20TH c.
Gourd, wood, animal skin
21 x 15 in.

Also called *zambomba,* this indigenous
drum is made from a large, hollow gourd
with a stick inserted through the middle of
the goatskin drumhead. By pushing and
pulling the stick, the player produces a
loud, low-register sound.

Did You Know?
During hunting, the Sumu people of
Honduras used a similar instrument
to flush out wildlife.

106

Kultrún (kettledrum)

MAPUCHE PEOPLE, LUMACO, ARAUCANÍA REGION, CHILE, 2009
Wood, goatskin
Luis Eugenio Leviñir Curaqueo, maker
7¾ x 15½ in.

This is the sacred drum of the *machi* (female shaman). Its motifs represent the cosmological world of the Mapuche. The *machi* places various symbolic objects inside, including feathers, rocks, medicinal herbs, and the hair of animals.

Panpipe (raft flute)

NAZCA PEOPLE, SOUTHERN COASTAL PERU, AD 100–600
Bone, alpaca fiber, human hair
7½ x 3 x ¾ in.

The Nazca made single- and double-row panpipes from bone and clay using great skill to tune intervals precisely. Players were often buried with their panpipe, with adornments added as signs of social status.

Rondador (raft flute)

ECUADOR, EARLY 20TH c.
Carrizo cane, textile
25 x 25½ x 1½ in.

Translated as "one who makes the rounds," this raft flute is named after the night watchmen of Quito who played this type of panpipe while making their rounds. Unlike panpipes of the central Andes, the zigzag setting of the *rondador*'s tubes allows the player to create harmonic effects at the ends of phrases by blowing two different-sized tubes at once.

Bajón (multiple trumpet)

BUENOS AIRES, ARGENTINA, c. 1996
Kusi palm leaves, wood
52 x 20 x 7 in.

Though similar in design to rafted flutes, the large *bajón* is a lip-vibrated multiple trumpet. This one is a reconstruction of an indigenous instrument from the San Ignacio de Moxos mission in Bolivia, used to play the bass in European-style music.

Vessel-whistle

VICUS PEOPLE, NORTHERN COASTAL PERU, 100 BC–AD 100
Ceramic
13 x 12 x 6 in.

This pre-Columbian double-chamber vessel-whistle depicts a panpipe player seated on top of a house. The instrument can be played by blowing into the opening of the mouthpiece on the "rear" chamber.

Did You Know?

Some pre-Columbian double-chamber vessels were designed to create whistling sounds when liquids were poured from them. The transfer of fluid between chambers created a change in air pressure that produced the sounds.

109

Trumpets

(left)
**MOCHE OR HUARI PEOPLE,
NORTH CENTRAL COASTAL PERU,
AD 600–700**
Wood, spondylus shell, turquoise
27 x 3¾ in.

(center)
**MOCHE PEOPLE, NORTHERN COASTAL
PERU, AD 100–300**
Copper, textile
64½ x 6¾ in.

(right)
**MOCHE PEOPLE, NORTHERN COASTAL
PERU, AD 300–500**
Ceramic, pigment
18½ x 3½ in.

MIM holds a collection of pre-Columbian musical instruments from the Andes, including rare ceremonial trumpets in different materials and a wide range of flute types built from reeds, modeled in ceramic, or carved in stone or bone. The instruments offer a glimpse of the South American past; their quality reflects the importance of musical traditions in the ritual and ceremonial lives of different ancient peoples.

Curator's Note

MIM's Moche copper trumpet is the largest one known of its kind. It was made using separate sections of copper sheet, cut to shape and bent to create the trumpet's form. The sections were then riveted and tied with textile thread. Fragments of the white thread are still visible on the trumpet.

Flutes

(top)
**CHIMÚ PEOPLE, NORTHERN
COASTAL PERU, AD 900–1400**
Bone, shell, jet
8¾ x 1¾ in.

(bottom)
**PARACAS PEOPLE, SOUTHERN
COASTAL PERU, 500–100 BC**
Bone, shell, jet
8½ x 1 in.

These pre-Columbian flutes display
sophisticated carvings of stylized
birds. On the Chimú example, which
features additional zoomorphic
motifs on its body, even the feet of
the bird are evident. These flutes
show significant wear and patina
from extensive use in antiquity, but
little is known of their original use.
Experts believe they were played
during shamanic rituals.

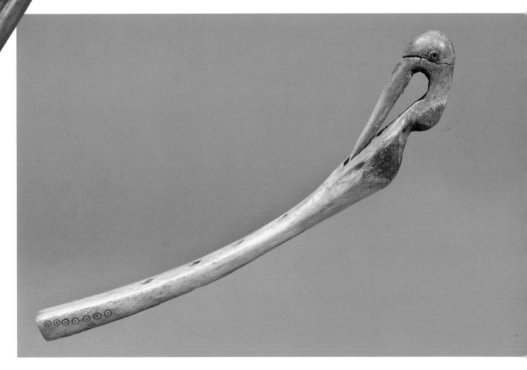

Tambores batá (double-headed hourglass drums)

HAVANA, CUBA, 1988
Roble wood, goatskin, rope, iron, textile
Juan Bencomo Pedroso, maker
19 x 8 in.; 23½ x 10 in.; 25 x 13½ in.

Pictured smallest to largest, the *okónkolo*, *itótele*, and *iyá* drums are played in ceremonies of the Santería religious tradition, which evolved from Nigerian Yorùbá and Spanish Catholic influences. The combination of six drumheads on the set of three instruments is used to create complex interlocking rhythms.

Congo hondo
(single-headed conical drum)

PORTOBELO, COLÓN PROVINCE, PANAMA, 20TH c.

Softwood, deerskin
19½ x 8 in.; 20 x 8½ in.; 18¾ x 7½ in.

The *congo hondo* is played in both the *conjunto típico* (typical ensemble) of Panama and in Afro-Panamanian drumming, where it is joined by a second *congo hondo* and a drum called a *repicador.* Once associated with Afro-Panamanian secret societies, the groups known as *Congos* today perform theatrical dances featuring bright, multicolored outfits, drumming, and responsorial singing.

Double-headed frame drum

NAZCA PEOPLE, SOUTHERN COASTAL PERU, AD 100–600

Wood, animal skin
4 x 10 in.

The arid conditions in southern Peru—where the Nazca people flourished—allowed this approximately 1,500-year-old drum to remain close to its original condition. Versions of the frame drum are found in use around the world. This example is made using multiple wooden slats to construct the frame; animal skins are then attached on both sides.

Did You Know?
The Nazcas are best known for their geoglyphs (also called Nazca Lines), desert earthworks that feature monumental figures and abstract forms. These can only be fully seen from high up in the air. How and why these figures were created is still subject to much speculation.

Guitarra chamula (plucked lute)

CHIAPAS HIGHLANDS, MEXICO, 20TH c.
Wood, nylon
31½ x 8½ x 3 in.
Ex Guillermo Contreras Arias Collection

The indigenous people of the Chiapas Highlands continue to protect their native traditions, yet blended in these are Spanish missionary influences from the 16th to 17th centuries, such as this guitar used to accompany songs of colonial origin revamped with Mayan musical flavor.

Berimbau
(musical bow with gourd resonator)

RIO DE JANEIRO, BRAZIL, 2009
Biriba wood, steel, gourd
Marcos China, maker
61⅝ x 8⁷⁄₁₆ x 12⅜ in.
5⅜ x 3¹⁄₁₆ x 2¹³⁄₁₆ in. (rattle)

The signature instrument of the Afro-Brazilian dance-sport capoeira, the *berimbau* has a gourd resonator and is played using a wooden stick with a basket rattle (*caxixi*). By utilizing a coin or stone as a bridge, the player of the *berimbau* produces two distinct pitches in rhythmic patterns that guide the singers and dancers.

Bandolim (plucked lute)

RIO DE JANEIRO, BRAZIL, 2009
Beech wood
Rogério Santos, maker
25⅜ x 12 x 2 3⁄16 in.

Similar to a mandolin, this eight-string Brazilian lute made by Rogério Santos is exemplary of those used as melody instruments in *choro* music. Brazil's parallel to American jazz, *choro* was dominated by Afro-Brazilian popular musicians in the early 20th century.

Did You Know?
Choro music earned its name from *chorões* or "weepers," ensembles of bohemian street musicians who performed dances and sentimental songs in 19th-century Rio de Janeiro.

Bandoneón (button accordion)

GERMANY, 1928
Wood, cardboard, metal, mother-of-pearl, leather
Alfred Arnold Co., maker
18 x 9¼ x 9¾ in.

The large button accordion invented by the German Heinrich Band in 1846 was noted for its unwieldy size and difficult fingering system. German and Italian emigrants brought it to the Americas, where it found great success as a solo instrument in tango orchestras in Argentina, Uruguay, and Brazil from about 1900. Originally associated with "seedy" characters, the music created a stir after tango musician Ástor Piazzola used the *bandoneón* in the 1953 debut of his classical orchestral composition, *Buenos Aires.*

Requinto (plucked lute)

ASUNCIÓN, PARAGUAY, 2009
Wood, metal, plastic
Constancio Sanabria, maker
34¾ x 14 x 5 in.

The Spanish-derived *requinto* is found in small ensembles of many Latin American countries, and its player assumes a lead role or provides a secondary, largely improvised, melodic line as a counterpoint to the singer or harpist. In Paraguay, popular ensembles of harp and guitars often add the *requinto*.

Cuatro (plucked lute)

MOROVIS, PUERTO RICO, 2009
Mahogany and pumpwood, steel, silk
Julio Negrón Rivera, maker
34⅜ x 11⅛ x 3⅞ in.

Named after its original four pairs of strings, this 10-string lute is emblematic of Puerto Rico's rural Hispanic music. The luthier Julio Negrón Rivera is one of the oldest and most revered carriers of the tradition.

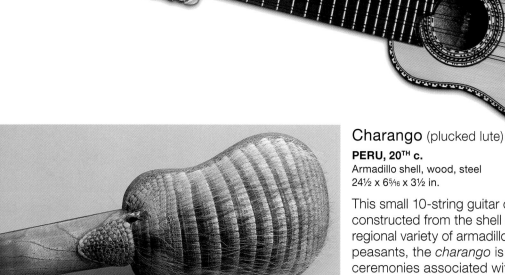

Charango (plucked lute)

PERU, 20TH c.
Armadillo shell, wood, steel
24½ x 6⁵⁄₁₆ x 3½ in.

This small 10-string guitar of Andean origin was constructed from the shell of the *quirquincho* (a regional variety of armadillo). Among indigenous peasants, the *charango* is played in seasonal ceremonies associated with the agricultural cycle. Young men also use the instrument in courting, performing melodies associated with romance.

Rámpora
(double-headed frame drum)

**RARÁMURI (TARAHUMARA) PEOPLE,
STATE OF CHIHUAHUA, MEXICO, 20TH c.**
Goatskin, wood, cord, textile
5½ x 28 in.

Played by dozens of "pharisees" during Easter ceremonies, the *rámpora* is then put away until the following year. By attaching a glass bead to a string stretched across the frame, a snare is made on one side of this drum. The red ochre decoration is made from clay containing iron oxide.

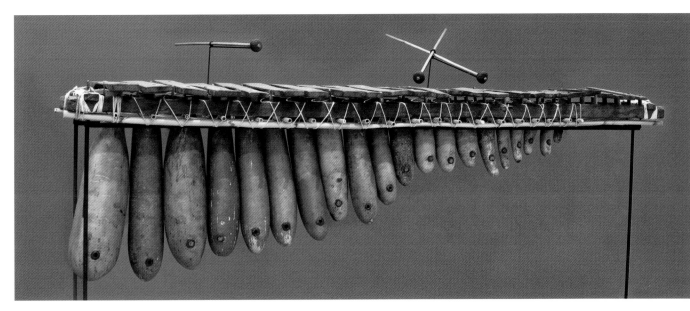

Marimba de tecomates (gourd-resonated xylophone)

GUATEMALA, 20TH c.
Wood, gourd
64 x 18 x 18½ in.

Of African origin but adopted and transformed by indigenous Americans and mestizos, the marimba was first observed in Guatemala in 1680 played by Mayan musicians in public festivities. This traditional marimba is called *sencilla* (simple) because it only has one keyboard. It is played at patron-saint celebrations and other ceremonial occasions, often accompanied by percussion, cane flute, or *chirmía* (a type of oboe).

Arpa grande (frame harp)

SAN DIEGO DE ISHUA, DEPARTMENT OF AYACUCHO, PERU, LATE 20TH c.
Wood
51⅞ x 25½ x 25 in.

Spanish missionaries propagated the harp throughout the Andean region, but indigenous musicians have made considerable adaptations to it. This harp of the Quechua people is a lightweight, portable instrument carried over the shoulder, fastened by two belts, and played upside down during processions and festivals. Along with the violin, it accompanies the *dansaq*, or "scissors dance."

Curator's Note

The scissors dance is a ritual battle of endurance between two specialists who perform spectacular acrobatic feats. As the violinist and harpist improvise a tune, the dancers' steps and the steel scissor-shaped clappers provide the rhythmic component to these compelling performances.

Old-time steel pan

KINGSTOWN, ST. VINCENT AND THE GRENADINES, MID-20TH c.
Steel
6 x 22½ in.

African descendants in the Caribbean invented a number of musical instruments. First were ensembles of bamboo stamping tubes. Then, starting in the late 1930s, steel pans were developed. Constructed from 55-gallon metal oil drums, the distinct pitches of the pan are made by an elaborate process of heating, hammering, and chiseling. From just a few simple musical tones in the early models to contemporary steel pans with more than 30 notes, clean bell-like sound, and a full ensemble of instruments from tenor to bass, the steel pan is one of the greatest inventions in musical instruments of the 20th century.

Stary Harp
("Instrument for Four Persons")

ST. ANN PARISH, JAMAICA, 20TH c.
Wood, metal, animal skin, plastic
Everald Brown, maker
66½ x 13½ x 35½ in.

This sculpture, by the noted Rastafarian artist and priest of the Ethiopian Orthodox Church known as "Brother Brown," is an exceptional piece illustrating the Rasta story through symbols of roots spirituality, peace, and unity, including the drum, guitar, harp, and metal tongues of the rhumba box as one instrument.

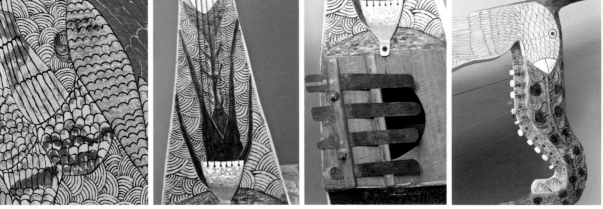

Elements with multiple ethnic roots, including *(left to right)* the colorful design, guitar body, rhumba box metal tongues, and harp strings are embraced in the Stary Harp, as they are in Jamaican music. The Stary Harp organically synthesizes the individual elements, uniting music with nature and our shared humanity.

The Argentina exhibit displays the emergence of a national music (tango) in urban centers as well as the preservation of diverse traditions of rural and indigenous peoples.

The Mexico exhibit shows how European harps, violins, and guitars inspired the creation of countless Mexican stringed instruments. These instruments are then combined in various regional styles of the *son,* a traditional genre of music and dance with strong presence in Mexican life.

(right) **The Brazil exhibit** portrays how the *atabaque* drum, strongly associated with neo-African ritual music, has become a symbol of the deep roots of African heritage in Brazil.

Brazil Exhibit

Viola d'amore from Bohemia, Czech Republic (page 131)

Europe Gallery

EUROPE

Albania
Andorra
Austria
Belarus
Belgium
Bosnia and Herzegovina
Bulgaria
Croatia
Cyprus
Czech Republic
Denmark
England
Estonia
Finland
France
Germany
Greece
Hungary
Iceland
Ireland
Italy
Kosovo
Latvia
Liechtenstein
Lithuania
Luxembourg
Macedonia
Malta
Moldova
Monaco
Montenegro
Netherlands
Norway
Poland
Portugal
Romania
Russia
San Marino
Scotland
Serbia
Slovakia
Slovenia
Spain
Sweden
Switzerland
Ukraine
Vatican City
Wales

MIM's Europe gallery encompasses the lands north of the Black Sea and west of the Ural Mountains in Russia, all the way to the Atlantic Ocean. It is bound by the Mediterranean Sea in the south and the Norwegian and Barents Seas in the north. Rural folk traditions and urban popular and classical musics flourish and influence each other, yielding a wealth of geographic diversity and historical change.

The Europe gallery showcases instruments from nearly fifty countries and city-states. The instruments and their music demonstrate an extensive European history of blending traditions among countries within the continent as well as with those in other regions of the world. As in the other galleries, the European exhibits demonstrate that region's use of both simple, functional instruments and exquisite, highly decorated ones.

Within the gallery, guests encounter several instances of traditions that were adapted from or influenced by non-European cultures. An interesting example is the bagpipe. Although most people associate bagpipes with Scotland, these instruments did not reach that country until the 1500s, long after they were in common use in the Middle East and North Africa. MIM's exhibits show an array of bagpipes from many countries within Europe and beyond.

The Ukraine exhibit contains instruments used in *tsimbaly* folk music ensembles—festive gatherings of the Hutsul people living in the Carpathian Mountains.

The Europe gallery showcases stories of connection, innovation, and discovery—from an antique charter horn to a foot-operated drum kit to a child's vessel flute.

Like the bagpipe, free reeds existed outside Europe for thousands of years, originally in Asia. They became popular in Europe in the early nineteenth century, when Europeans adopted and adapted the principle of vibrating free reeds to create such varied instruments as harmonicas, accordions, and reed organs. A popular instrument in MIM's Europe gallery, the six-string hurdy-gurdy, or "wheel fiddle," has Eastern Byzantine origins, and found its way into European minstrelsy through Spain. Although commonly associated with street musicians, beggars, or peasants, the hurdy-gurdy enjoyed favor with the French aristocracy in the eighteenth century.

One of the largest exhibits in the gallery comprises instruments of a nineteenth-century symphony orchestra, which had its beginnings in eighteenth-century Baroque courts and churches. The historic strings, woodwinds, brasswinds, and percussion instruments in this display form the basis of the modern orchestra. The increasing popularity of public concerts during the classical period (1750–1830) led to the orchestra's tripling in size. Instrument innovations gave composers an expanded musical vocabulary and allowed them to create new, groundbreaking works. A *cor anglais* (tenor oboe) made

127

The Germany exhibit highlights innovations in instrument design and manufacture, such as the development of valves for brass instruments. The exhibit also includes Renaissance-inspired instruments crafted during a post–World War II revival of early music in Germany.

by August Grenser in Germany around 1760, a viola crafted in France about 1775, and an oboe completed by Gottfried August Lehnold in Germany around 1800 are just a few of the fine instruments displayed in this exhibit.

Instrumental innovation also led to the establishment of new forms of music. The Belgian-born Adolphe Sax was the inventor of the saxophone and the saxhorn family of brasswind instruments. Although the saxophone and brasswinds were originally intended for use in the Paris opera, they were adopted by and played by the French army. Sax's inventions created sounds that eventually would prove to be pivotal components of many new genres.

The Europe gallery also features an ethnic group whose musical customs have traveled with them for centuries. The nomadic Roma people (commonly known as Gypsies) have roamed the length and breadth of Europe for generations, often serving as the musicians for other cultures. The Roma have influenced many forms of European music with their rich and flexible styles, and they have inspired and influenced a variety of genres such as urban jazz.

The Europe gallery showcases stories of connection, innovation, and discovery—from an antique charter horn to a foot-operated drum kit to a child's vessel flute. Some of these stories are familiar, others less well-known; some are fraught with politics and ethnic conflict, while still others show immense cultural achievements. Zithers, drums, pipes, flutes, and fiddles of all shapes, sizes, and materials fill the gallery. All demonstrate that people in Europe, just as others across the globe, have felt the need to continually create instruments as amplifiers of human emotion.

Instruments of the
Europe Gallery

Clavicytherium
(harpsichord)

GOUDHURST, KENT, ENGLAND, 1979
Wood, metal, parchment, ebony, felt, paint
Adlam & Burnett, maker
55 x 25¼ x 8 in.

This upright harpsichord is a replica of the oldest existing keyboard instrument, a southern German *clavicytherium* (c. 1480). The original instrument is housed in the Royal College of Music in London.

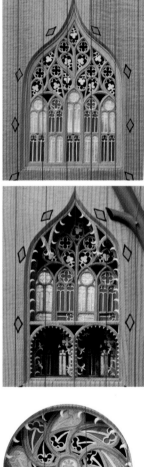

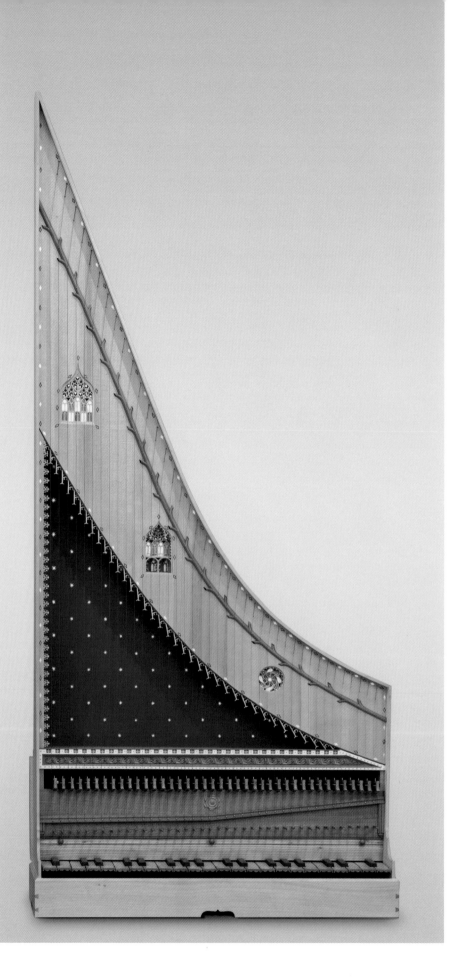

Viola d'amore (bowed lute)

**BOHEMIA, CZECH REPUBLIC,
1730–1750**
Maple, spruce, and ebony woods;
metal; mother-of-pearl
31 x 9½ x 4½ in.
*Ex Fiske Collection,
Claremont University Consortium*

Although the specific maker is
uncertain, this instrument was
made according to the Prague
School style. This "viol of love"
has seven strings that are
bowed and seven that resonate
sympathetically. The distinctive
shape of this viola's sound
holes is called "flaming swords."

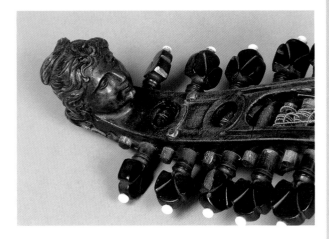

Did You Know?
The Italian composer Antonio
Vivaldi is one of the most
famous composers to have
written music for this instrument.

Woodwind instruments of the classical period, played during the time of Mozart and Haydn, have few or no keys. This is illustrated by the four instruments seen here—woodwinds that could have been played together in a classical-period orchestra. This group includes an extremely rare type of curved tenor oboe, commonly referred to as an English horn (*cor anglais*), made by August Grenser. The curved body lessens the distance between finger holes, facilitating playing ease. Over time, the English horn gained more keys; its body became angled and then straight.

Cor anglais
(double-reed pipe)

DRESDEN, SAXONY, GERMANY, c. 1760
Wood, leather, brass
August Grenser, maker
23½ x 2¾ in.
Ex Fiske Collection, Claremont University Consortium

Flute (side-blown flute)

POTSDAM, BRANDENBURG, GERMANY, c. 1790
Palisander wood, ivory, brass
Friedrich Gabriel August Kirst, maker
24 x 1½ in.
Ex Fiske Collection, Claremont University Consortium

Curator's Note
An "English horn" is neither English nor a horn, but a double-reed pipe that probably originated in Germany. Scholars speculate that the name is a translation of the Middle German *Englischhorn* (which could mean both "English horn" and "angelic horn"). "Angelic" may refer to the sweet, mellow sound produced by the addition of the bulb-shaped bell.

Clarinet in C (single-reed pipe)
PARIS, FRANCE, c. 1785
Boxwood, ivory, brass
Pierre Naust, maker
21¼ x 3 in.
*Ex Fiske Collection,
Claremont University
Consortium*

Oboe (double-reed pipe)
**LEIPZIG, SAXONY,
GERMANY, c. 1800**
Boxwood, ivory, brass
Gottfried August Lehnhold, maker
22¾ x 2½ in.
*Ex Fiske Collection,
Claremont University Consortium*

Mandolino (plucked lute)
NAPLES, CAMPANIA, ITALY, 1763
Wood, tortoiseshell, metal, ivory, mother-of-pearl
Joanies Vinaccia, maker
21 x 7¼ x 4¾ in.
Ex Fiske Collection, Claremont University Consortium

Made by a member of the most prominent mandolin-making family in Naples, this bowl-backed model is a typical southern Italian design with eight metal strings. The southern playing technique is characterized by a rapid tremolo picking style.

Vielle à roue (wheel fiddle)

ROUEN, UPPER NORMANDY, FRANCE, LATE 18th c.
Wood, ivory, iron, ink
Noel Morin, maker
32¼ x 12 x 8½ in.

This instrument is named for its wheel, which, when cranked by the right hand, sets the strings in vibration; essentially, it is a mechanically bowed (and keyed) fiddle. This lovely example is ornamented with birds and flowers and has a decorative pattern on the ribs and key-box lid that imitates tortoiseshell. This *vielle* is likely made in imitation of instruments found at the French court before the Revolution.

Curator's Note

Although today we often associate the *vielle à roue*, commonly called a hurdy-gurdy, with peasants, it was only after the French Revolution that this instrument was played by folk musicians.

Lyre guitar (plucked lute)

FRANCE, c. 1815
Maple, spruce, and ebony woods; brass; mother-of-pearl; gut; ivory
33¼ x 17¼ x 4⅞ in.

Guitars inspired by the form of Greek lyres were fashionable among ladies in salons during the French Empire period, when neoclassical styles were favored in decorations and furniture.

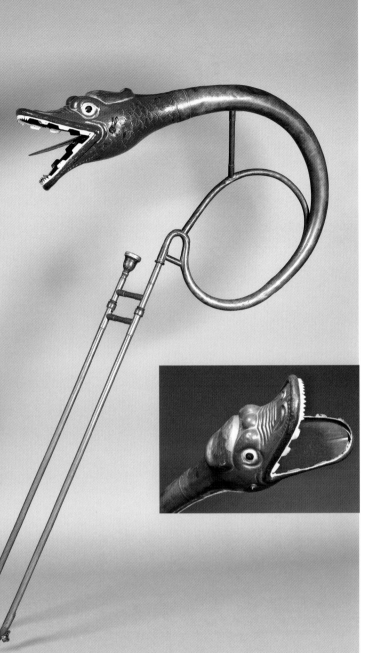

Buccin (slide trombone)

LYON, FRANCE, 1820–1848
Brass
Jean-Baptiste Tabard, maker
(slide made by A. K. Hüttl)
32½ x 4⅝ x 1⁷⁄₁₆ in. (body)
27 x 17 x 5½ in. (slide)
Ex Fiske Collection,
Claremont University Consortium

Basson russe (bass horn)

LYON, FRANCE, 1820–1848
Wood, brass
Jean-Baptiste Tabard, maker
45 x 14 x 5 in.
Ex Fiske Collection,
Claremont University Consortium

Used in French military ensembles during the first half of the 19th century, trombones and horns with colorfully painted zoomorphic heads were likely intended to inspire awe in listeners. The serpent head of this *buccin* is complete with an articulated tongue that moves freely while the performer marches.

Curator's Note

This *basson russe* is neither "Russian" nor a "bassoon," but a bass horn. It has been suggested that the name may be a misnomer stemming from a Lyonnais maker named Rust, combined with the instrument's bassoon-like appearance.

135

Nouveau alto (alto valved horn)

PARIS, FRANCE, 1866
Brass
Adolphe Sax, maker
28½ x 14¾ x 4½ in.

Around 1843, Adolphe Sax developed saxhorns to be played at the Paris Opera, where he was director. Also adopted by French military bands, his "new saxhorns" had peculiar valves and a rotating bell. This is one of the few examples of this model outside of Europe.

Guitarra portuguesa (plucked lute)

PORTO, PORTUGAL, 1880–1914
Wood, metal, mother-of-pearl
Custódio Cardoso Pereira & Companhia, maker
27 x 11⅛ x 4⅜ in.

A descendant of the medieval *cittole* and Renaissance cittern, the Portuguese guitar today is most commonly associated with fado. Fado is a dramatically melancholic vocal tradition that originated during the 1820s in the city of Coimbra in Portugal. In the fado tradition, a singer is accompanied by both a Portuguese and a classical guitar. MIM's *guitarra portuguesa* bears the characteristic fan-shaped tuning mechanisms, sometimes called "peacock" tuners.

Viola da gamba (bowed lute)

MILAN, ITALY, c. 1895
Wood, metal
Leandro Bisiach, maker
25½ x 9 x 4¾ in.
Ex Fiske Collection, Claremont University Consortium

This is a beautiful replica of a 16th-century tenor viol. The original, made by Giovanni Maria da Brescia, is part of the Hill Collection, Ashmolean Museum, Oxford, England. The instrument is played in an upright position on the player's legs (*gamba* means "leg" in Italian), as opposed to playing it "on the arm" (a viola "*da braccio*"), like a violin.

Oliphant (trumpet)

ENGLAND, LATE 19TH c.
Ivory
34 x 3 in.

Since medieval times, "charter horns" such as this one have been sounded to mark the transference of land ownership. The carvings on this elephant-tusk horn depict elaborate hunting scenes.

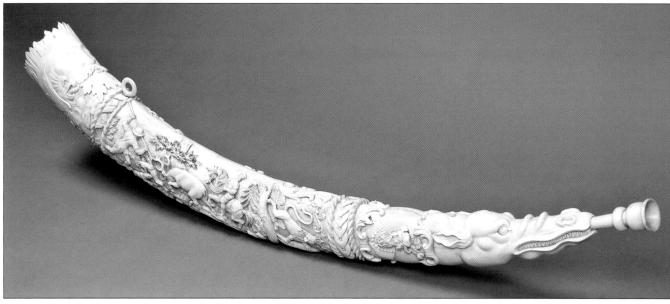

Harmoschka (button accordion)

SHUYA, RUSSIA, LATE 20TH c.
Wood, metal, celluloid
9 x 8¼ x 5 in.

Perepelochka (zither)

BELARUS, LATE 20TH c.
Wood, metal
14¾ x 8 x 1³⁄₁₆ in.
Ex René Grémaux Collection

Svistulka (vessel flute)

RUSSIA, LATE 20TH c.
Wood
3⅛ x 1⁹⁄₁₆ x 3⅜ in.
Ex René Grémaux Collection

This group of children's instruments from Eastern Europe includes a small accordion, zither, and ocarina or vessel flute. Cyrillic characters on the accordion, decorated with a flower design on its red celluloid exterior, spell *schul,* a derivation of the German word for school. The name of the zither, *perepelochka*, has a similar association with childhood—the word means "little quail" in Belorussian. The third instrument, a hand-painted vessel flute, features bright colors and fine detail. The flute sounds a single pitch when blown.

Accordéon chromatique
(button accordion)

PARIS, FRANCE, 1946
Wood, plastic, cardboard, celluloid, metal, leather
Buzzi Frères, maker
13 x 17 x 9½ in.

This instrument was previously owned by
bal musician Marcel Theuriot. In 2008, it
was used in the French film *Faubourg 36.*

Batterie mécanique
(mechanical drum kit)

TULLE, CORRÈZE, FRANCE, 1920s
Wood, animal skin, metal
*Bergerault (Ligueil) or Coquoz (Paris),
possible maker*
35 x 27³⁄₁₆ x 14 in.

Accordionists play this foot-operated instrument to
accompany themselves. Distributed by Maugein Frères, it is
decorated with "LuLu Jazz," the name of the band that used
it. This instrument dates from the 1920s, when jazz began to
be popular in France.

Pandero quadrat
(double-headed frame drum)

CATALONIA, SPAIN, 2009
Pinewood, goatskin, oil paint, silk
Albert Margalef Amorós, maker
Josep Quesada Cortés, artist
4¼ x 23 x 22½ in.

This two-sided painted drum is a replica of an instrument (c. 1920) in the Salvador Vilaseca Regional Museum in Tarragona, Spain. It features a different painting on each side. The original was played to accompany dance songs and Catholic feast-day processionals of the Majorales del Roser sisterhood.

Fujara (duct flute)

(top)
SLOVAKIA, LATE 20ᵀᴴ c.
Maple wood, brass, aluminum, leather
Dusan Sur, maker
34⅜ x 1⅝ x 2⅛ in.

Fujara (duct flute)

(bottom)
BANSKÁ BYSTRICA REGION, SLOVAKIA, 2008
Elder wood, leather
Tibor L. Kobliček, maker
67½ x 2⅜ x 3¼ in.

The *fujara* is a contrabass overtone flute that can be over five and a half feet long. Although the flute has only three finger holes, players use a technique called "overblowing," which allows them to obtain a fuller range of pitches. This technique gives the *fujara* its characteristic breathy tone. Originally a shepherd's instrument, it has become an iconic folk instrument of Slovakia.

Tambor
(double-headed cylindrical drum)

PRINCIPALITY OF ASTURIAS, SPAIN, 2002
Walnut wood, goatskin, rope, goat gut,
leather, metal
Andresín d'Insiertu, maker
10½ x 14 in.

Gaita (bagpipe)

GALICIA, SPAIN, 1985
Textile, calfskin, grenadillo wood, cow horn, reed
Xosé Lois Vázquez Carracedo, maker
46½ x 18 x 4 in.

The Spanish *gaita* is a type of bagpipe
that has persisted since the Middle
Ages. In a number of European
traditions, bagpipes are coupled with
different types of drums, like the *tambor*
seen here.

"Mark VI" tenor saxophone
(single-reed pipe)

PARIS, FRANCE, 1970
Brass, lacquer, leather, cork, plastic
Henri Selmer Paris, maker
31 x 6 x 10½ in.

The Mark VI was available for a limited time in a number of factory-finished colors, including this one—a striking pink-colored lacquer. The Mark VI, arguably Selmer's greatest saxophone model, has been played by many renowned musicians, including Stan Getz and John Coltrane.

Kromatisk nyckelharpa
(keyed fiddle)

UPPLAND, SWEDEN, 1984
Wood, metal
Eric Sahlström, maker
36 x 8¾ x 5⅜ in.

Interest in the *nyckelharpa*, a centuries-old instrument with Scandinavian origins, experienced a revival beginning in the 1960s. This was due in large part to the musical and technical innovations of Eric Sahlström (1912–1986). Nowadays the instrument may be heard in both popular and traditional music. The chromatic *nyckelharpa* pictured here has three rows of keys and a bow with a characteristic curve near the tip.

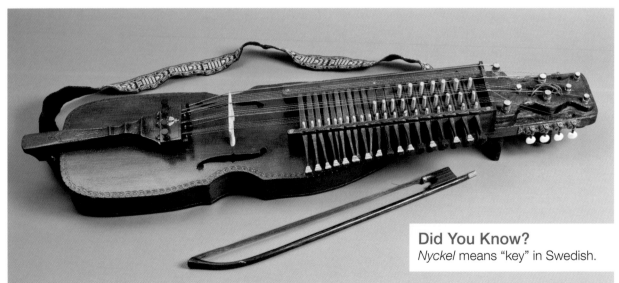

Did You Know?
Nyckel means "key" in Swedish.

Tenora (shawm)

CATALONIA, SPAIN, 1992
Jujube wood, brass, nickel
silver, ebony, reed, plastic
Miguel Puigdellívol, maker
35¹/₁₆ x 4¹⁵/₁₆ in.

The *cobla de sardana* is a Catalan wind-
instrument band that accompanies a spirited
folk dance called the *sardana.* The *cobla* has
medieval origins and, today, includes a highly
distinctive instrumentation.

Tible (shawm)

CATALONIA, SPAIN, 1989
Jujube and cherry woods,
brass, plastic, reed
Miguel Puigdellívol, maker
21¹/₁₆ x 2³/₁₆ in.

"Esportazione Modale" fiscorn
(valved horn)

MILAN, LOMBARDY, ITALY, c. 1920
Brass
Rampone & Cazzani, maker
20¼ x 11¼ x 7⅞ in.

Flabiol de cobla
(duct flute)

**CATALONIA, SPAIN,
LATE 1970s**
Ebony wood
Pau Orriols, maker
9½ x 1¼ in.

Tamborí de cobla
(double-headed cylindrical drum
and beater)

CATALONIA, SPAIN, 2009
Wood, goatskin, metal
5 x 4½ in.

The World of Bagpipes exhibit highlights a rich assortment of 19ᵗʰ- and 20ᵗʰ-century bagpipes from countries around the world, such as Italy, Poland, and Tunisia.

The Russia exhibit showcases folk instruments from the *domra* and *balailaika* families, instruments resembling those played in the national folk orchestra of the late 19ᵗʰ century.

(right) **The *octobasse* in MIM's Orientation Gallery** is a rare bowed lute that stands over 12 feet tall. It is a modern version of an instrument (c. 1850) made by the famed Jean-Baptiste Vuillaume. The player must stand on a stool and use a series of levers to "finger" different notes. Made by Antonio Datis in 2007, it is one of only a few such instruments in the world.

NG MUSICAL

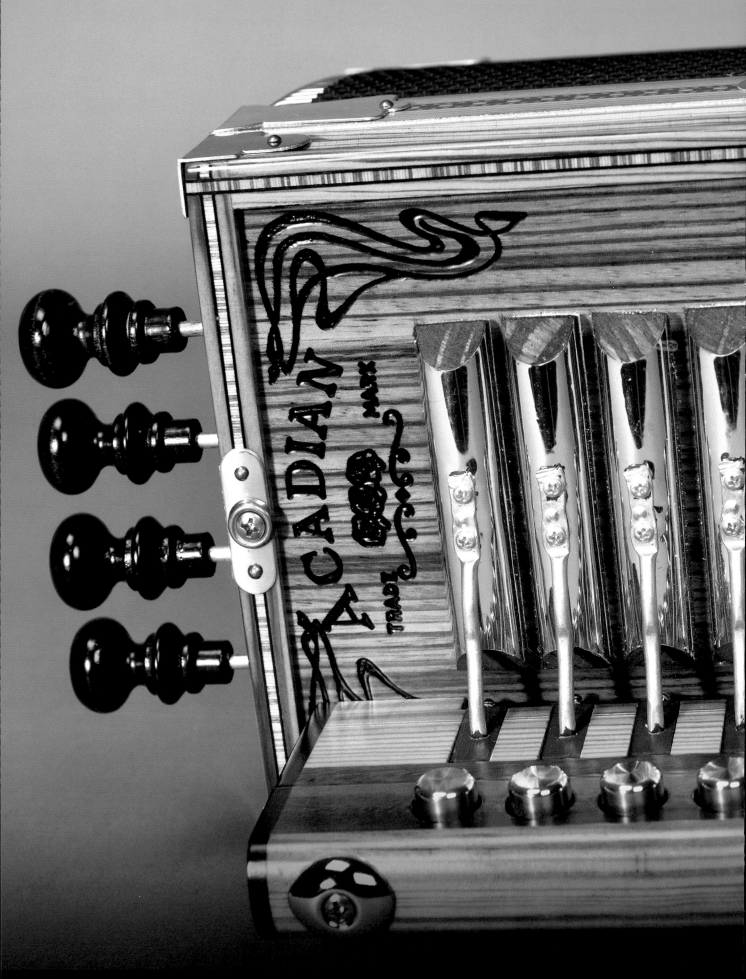

Cajun accordion from Louisiana, USA (page 165)

United States / Canada
Gallery

UNITED STATES / CANADA
Exhibit Themes

African Arrivals
All-American Bands
Appalachia
Arizona Artists
Banjos
Bluegrass
Blues
Brass Trumpets
Cajun
Canadian Fiddle Traditions
Conjunto
Country
Dixieland
Domestic Music
Drum Set
Electronic Music
Fife and Drum
Folk Revival
Fretless Zithers
Grand Harmonicon
Hammond B-3
Handbells
Hawaiian Music
Hip Hop
Instrument Makers
Jazz
Klezmer
Latin Jazz
Mail Order Instruments
Mandolin Orchestra
Marching Band
Native American Musical Traditions
Norteño
Polka
Ragtime
Rock and Roll
Salsa
The Stick
String Band
Taiko
Zydeco

Representing most of North America, MIM's United States / Canada gallery highlights many musical genres. The gallery features instruments from indigenous peoples as well as instruments that reflect interactions with Europeans, Africans, and immigrants from other regions of the globe.

Powerhouses of musical invention, the United States and Canada are represented in MIM's largest Geographical Gallery. Waves of immigration over the course of four centuries have resulted in the blending of diverse musical traditions in these two vast countries, creating a complex and ever-changing tapestry of sound and style. At MIM, guests enjoy exhibits highlighting musical genres, notable instruments, and innovative manufacturers.

A significant portion of the United States / Canada gallery is devoted to indigenous peoples. Although tribal customs remain distinct, more than five hundred Native American tribes across North America share musical links. Fundamental elements of Native American music include the use of the human voice as a key instrument, a strong connection between music and dance, a range of percussion instruments and flutes, and an enduring association with ceremony and ritual. Native Americans foster strong relationships between

The Steinway Piano Workshop exhibit features an "exploded piano" that affords a unique look inside the instrument.

Waves of immigration over the course of four centuries have resulted in the blending of diverse musical traditions in these two vast countries, creating a complex and ever-changing tapestry of sound and style.

sound and movement; dancers often use bird beaks, deer hooves, and turtle shells as rattles in performances. The gallery showcases the essential union of music, dance, and instruments constructed with inherited knowledge and carried forward by today's performers.

Other exhibits reflect ways in which indigenous peoples have interacted with newcomers to produce original genres rooted in the Old World. South Texas conjunto, for example, fused Czech, German, and Polish musical styles with songs and ballads from Northern Mexico. In the Southwest borderland, European settlers and Catholic missionaries introduced the fiddle and accordion to the Tohono O'odham people, who used these instruments in creating the vibrant social dance music called *waila*, or "chicken scratch."

The musical traditions and innovations of African slaves and their descendants likewise resulted in distinct North American sounds. African slaves in the New World used available materials to reinvent traditional instruments; the sounds of their singing and playing have powered American music for generations. Following the abolition of slavery in the South in 1865, the vital African-American presence led to early string-band music, blues, jazz, and rock and roll, as well as

The All-American Bands exhibit contains a one-of-a-kind set of seven over-the-shoulder horns by Hall & Quinby of Boston. These instruments were constructed to project sound behind the player to the marching soldiers following the band.

to zydeco, hip hop, and other uniquely American genres represented in the gallery.

In addition to genres, MIM features many individual North American instruments of historical significance. The rationing of metals during World War II is reflected by a 1944 Ludwig "Victory" drum set, fashioned almost entirely from wood. The iconic 1934 "Frying Pan" guitar was the first electric string instrument to earn commercial success. The 1831 grand harmonicon comes from a time when parlor music was especially popular among amateur musicians. Further illuminating links to the past are exhibits devoted to key North American instrument brands such as Steinway, Martin, and Fender. These "workshop" displays trace connections between Old World traditions and New World advances in technology, materials, and design.

Specifically highlighting Arizona's musical past is a portion of the gallery celebrating the state's centennial. MIM's first self-produced special exhibition, *I Am AZ Music*, features musicians, musical instrument makers, recording studios, performing arts organizations, and musical traditions significant to Arizona's past, present, and future.

The musical ideas and instruments that have traveled to North America throughout its history encouraged fluid, constantly evolving creativity. The fusion and reinvention of these distinct legacies from around the world have created in the United States and Canada a musical landscape unlike any other. From the familiar to the fantastical, the objects in the United States / Canada gallery will introduce guests to a region rich in music history and style.

Instruments of the
United States /
Canada Gallery

Curator's Note

Musical glasses saw a decline around 1860 with rumors that playing the instrument caused madness, because many players suffered nervous breakdowns. At the time, it was thought that the vibrations resulted in nervous system decline, but it may be that touching the glasses and their painted rims—both of which contained lead—contributed to lead poisoning over time.

Grand harmonicon (musical glasses)

BALTIMORE, MARYLAND, USA, 1831
Wood, crystal, metal
Francis H. Smith, maker
36 x 58 x 34¼ in.
Ex Fiske Collection, Claremont University Consortium

The grand harmonicon is an array of tuned drinking glasses, each blown to pitch and placed on a sounding board for resonance. The instrument is played by running a moistened finger around the rims of the glasses. Patented in 1825, the grand harmonicon was intended primarily for use at home rather than in a concert hall; it was sold with an accompanying method book that contained transcriptions of popular music.

Snare drum

CHICAGO, ILLINOIS, USA, 1908
Wood, metal, calfskin
Lyon & Healy, maker
11½ x 17½ in.
Loan courtesy of Christopher Siegle in memory of Richard L. Siegle

Inlaid with several types of wood and still bearing its original calfskin heads, this presentation piece was commissioned as a prize for a 1908 drum competition in Chicago. The lender's grandfather, Robert A. Siegle, won the instrument at the age of 12.

Marking piano and console

DEKALB, ILLINOIS, USA, EARLY 20TH c.
Wood, metal
Melville Clark Piano Co., maker
75½ x 58 x 40 in. (piano)
36 x 41½ x 22 in. (console)
Loan courtesy of QRS Music Technologies, Inc.

This instrument recorded hand-played piano rolls with its carbon-marking console at QRS Music Company from 1912 to 1931 and later from 1972 to 1996. Legendary pianists Blind Boone, James P. Johnson, and Fats Waller all recorded rolls on this instrument, significantly shaping the development of ragtime and early jazz.

Tsii' edo' atl (fiddle)

APACHE PEOPLE, BYLAS, ARIZONA, USA, 1915–1945
Century plant, pigment, textile
Amos Gustina, maker
21¾ x 10½ x 5 in.

Commonly called an Apache violin or fiddle, this instrument is played during social occasions and as part of important ceremonies. It is said to be a native adaptation of instruments brought into the Southwest by European settlers. Its type may relate to musical bows and other similar string instruments found in northern Mexico, where Apache once held territories.

Curator's Note
The native name for this instrument translates as "singing wood" or "wood that sings."

Rasp and gourd resonator

HOPI PEOPLE, ARIZONA, USA, 20TH c.
Wood, gourd, fiber
7½ x 26 x 10½ in.

Hopi traditional belief maintains that people, plants, and all material things, along with the spiritual or the supernatural, interact rhythmically as part of a universal sense of order. To connote a sense of sharing and community balance, rasps of this type may be used ceremonially to correlate the act of playing the instrument with women's practice of grinding corn.

Liberty model miniature trumpet

CLEVELAND, OHIO, USA, 1930–1932
Brass
The H. N. White Co., maker
12⅜ x 3¾ in.
Ex Fiske Collection, Claremont University Consortium

The smallest trumpet in MIM's collection and one of fewer than 100 ever made, this fully playable instrument is exactly half the size and one octave higher than the normal Liberty model no. 1 trumpet. Lore holds that it was built for and played by jazz trumpeter Clyde McCoy, who was known for "Sugar Blues" and a slew of other hits.

Did You Know?
A cofounder of *DownBeat* magazine, Clyde McCoy was from the McCoy line of the Hatfield-McCoy feud fame.

Liberty model bass trumpet

CLEVELAND, OHIO, USA, 1925–1930
Brass
The H. N. White Co., maker
94 x 14½ in.
Ex Fiske Collection, Claremont University Consortium

In stark contrast to its miniature cousin and even rarer, this tuba in trumpet form is also a version of the Liberty model no. 1 trumpet.

155

Marxolin
(bowed and struck zither)

NEW TROY, MICHIGAN, USA, 1930–1950
Wood, metal
Marxochime Colony, maker
20 x 7 x 4 in.
Gift of Garry Harrison

A testament to the seemingly endless varieties of American fretless zithers, this futuristic invention calls for an extremely determined player. The instrument consists of two stacked bodies and is played with a bow containing two separate ribbons of horsehair. The base of the zither contains a tremolo bar, a set of spring hammers that strike chords, and two levers that raise the pitch of several strings at once.

1191PV "Victory" drum set

CHICAGO, ILLINOIS, USA, 1944
Wood, plastic, metal
Ludwig & Ludwig, maker
49 x 40 x 40 in. (assembled)

With the onset of World War II, President Franklin D. Roosevelt established the War Production Board (WPB) to regulate American manufacturing resources. Metal was in high demand for war-related products, and the WPB strictly limited the amount of metal used in "nonessential" items, such as this drum set. Many parts that would typically be made of metal—like the rims and some of the hardware on the drum's outer shell—are made of wood on this instrument.

ES-250 (electric guitar)

KALAMAZOO, MICHIGAN, USA, 1940
Wood, metal
Gibson, Inc., maker
42 x 17 x 5½ in.
Loan courtesy of Lynn Wheelwright

Charlie Christian used this instrument to pave the way for solo electric-guitar playing in jazz music. Voted best guitarist by *DownBeat* magazine for three consecutive years, Christian played this ES-250 with the Benny Goodman Sextet and posed with it on the cover of the album *Solo Flight: The Genius of Charlie Christian.*

Rickenbacher A-22
"Frying Pan" (electric guitar)

LOS ANGELES, CALIFORNIA, USA, 1934
Aluminum, metal, plastic
Electro String Corp., maker
29 x 6⅞ x 2½ in.

Nicknamed for its looks, the "Frying Pan" is one of the most historically important 20th-century guitars. It was the first solid-body guitar as well as the first commercially successful electrified string instrument, and this particular example is among the first ever built. Its sound quality still rivals all other steel guitars, especially when played through its accompanying amplifier—historically significant in its own right.

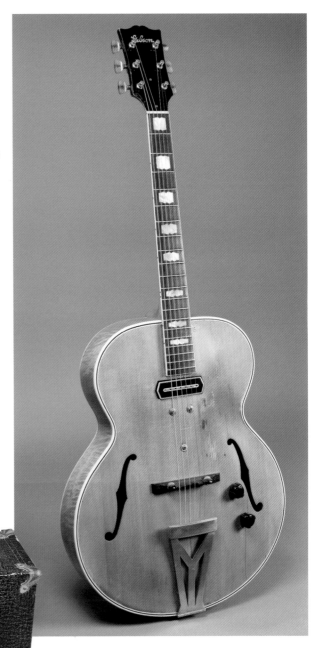

157

Native American flute

SAC AND FOX (MESQUAKIE) PEOPLES, TAMA, IOWA, USA, 1950s
Wood, suede
20 x 1¾ x 3½ in.

This instrument features two interior air chambers separated by an inner wall, with air flowing through the resonator chamber (near the mouthpiece) and a sound chamber (flute's body), using a "block" or "totem" to control the transfer of air between chambers. This flute's block is carved in the shape of a horse, a historically important animal for many Native American peoples.

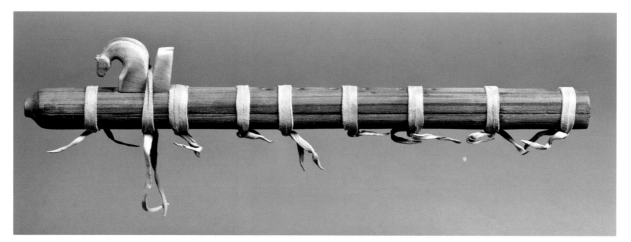

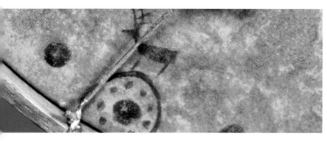

Frame drum

NASKAPI (INNU) PEOPLE, SHESHATSHIU, NEWFOUNDLAND AND LABRADOR, CANADA, MID-20TH c.
Animal skin, birch, pigment
2¾ x 13 in.

The "remote" Naskapi became historically known as "people beyond the horizon," reflecting the fact that they mostly remained outside European missionary reach in their far northern territories. There they hunted caribou, moose, and deer, and they trapped beaver for trade. This single-headed drum retains an attached string with small pegs that served as a snare. It features painted bird and caribou or elk motifs, pertinent to songs celebrating the hunt and the Naskapi way of life.

"Mark VI" alto saxophone
(single-reed pipe)

PARIS, FRANCE, 1955
Brass, mother-of-pearl
Henri Selmer Paris, maker
28⅜ x 4¾ x 7½ in.

Because of its desirable tone and design, the Mark VI has enjoyed a spot among the top professionally played saxophones for decades.

Curator's Note
This horn was formerly owned and played by Fernando Joaquin of the Joaquin Brothers, one of the finest Tohono O'odham bands performing the polka-rooted social dance music called *waila* or "chicken scratch," which originated in the Sonoran Desert of Southern Arizona.

"BB-4 Baby Bass"
(electric upright bass)

WOODINVILLE, WASHINGTON, USA, 1966–1972
Plastic, wood, metal
Ampeg, maker
62 x 20 x 12 in.

An early electric upright bass known as the Zorko bass was developed by Rudy and Ed Dopera in the late 1950s. Ampeg bought the rights to the Zorko and, with a few modifications, began producing and selling their Baby Bass models in the 1960s. This versatile instrument is at home in Afro-Cuban music and polka alike.

National "Glenwood 95"
(electric guitar)

CHICAGO, ILLINOIS, USA, 1962
Fiberglass, wood, metal
Valco Manufacturing Co., maker
40¼ x 15¼ x 2¾ in.

Valco was one of the first guitar manufacturers to build instruments with bodies made of materials other than wood. The company used Res-O-Glas (a trade name for fiberglass) for this "map guitar" from the early 1960s. The body's stylized shape resembles a map of the United States.

"Baldwin Crossover"
(pedal steel guitar)

NASHVILLE, TENNESSEE, USA, 1970
Wood, metal, celluloid
Sho-Bud Guitar Co., maker
33¾ x 12⅜ x 49½ in.

The pedal steel is a development of the Hawaiian lap steel guitar. The foot and knee pedals of the Crossover allow musicians to loosen and tighten strings while playing, and an additional lever joins the pedals to one of the instrument's two necks. These mechanical components, when combined with fingerpicks in one of the player's hands and a smooth, metal bar in the other hand, result in the complex gliding and bending of pitches and chords so characteristic of country music and a growing number of other genres.

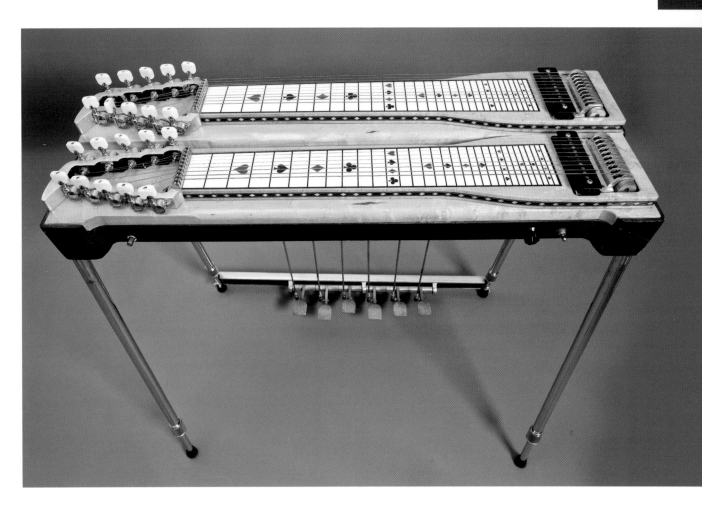

Did You Know?
The Sho-Bud Guitar Company was named for its two founders, steel guitarists Shot Jackson and Buddy Emmons. Hearts, spades, diamonds, and clubs became famous design features on their instruments.

Nudie suit

NORTH HOLLYWOOD, CALIFORNIA, USA, 1972
Cotton, suede, leather
Nudie's Rodeo Tailors, maker
Créations Isabelle de Borchgrave,
mannequin design
43½ x 16 x 2 in.

Nudie Cohn was famous for making glitzy stage outfits for country music stars. This rather modest example was made for Jon McIntire, manager of the Fillmore West and the Grateful Dead.

Curator's Note

The mannequin seen here is one of many that were custom-made for MIM at the studio Créations Isabelle de Borchgrave in Brussels, Belgium. The works of artist and designer de Borchgrave have been exhibited in museums around the world.

"Precision Bass" (electric bass guitar)

FULLERTON, CALIFORNIA, USA, 1973
Wood, metal
Fender Musical Instruments, maker
46 x 12¾ x 2¾ in.

Introduced in the early 1950s, the revolutionary Precision Bass (or "P-bass") had frets—metal bars along the neck—that made intonation more precise than on the traditional fretless acoustic upright bass. The P-bass also met demands for a bass that could rival the volume of the electric guitar, and it still enjoys widespread use among bassists in numerous genres. The instrument seen here is a left-handed model.

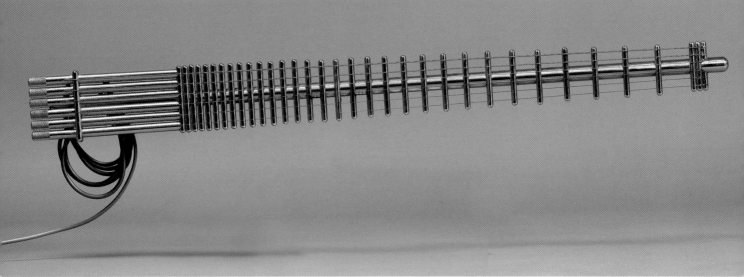

Did You Know?
Andy Summers played a Gittler guitar in the Police's 1983 music video *Synchronicity II.*

Gittler guitar (electric guitar)

NEW YORK, NEW YORK, USA, 1970–1985
Metal
Allan Gittler, maker
29 x 3 x ¾ in.

The maker of this electric guitar considered it to be a bare-bones, purely functional instrument containing no unnecessary parts. Its design uses tubular stainless steel and allows for tuning with precision beyond what conventional guitars offer.

Button accordion

HOUSTON, TEXAS, USA, 1965–1969
Wood, pearloid/celluloid, hard plastic, metal, leather, Swarovski crystals
Gabbanelli Accordions, maker
16 x 14 x 8½ in.

Italian immigrant Gianfranco "John" Gabbanelli recognized a market for colorful, highly decorated accordions. His instruments, like this green example adorned with Swarovski crystals, have become popular with players of many border styles, including norteño and conjunto.

Bajo sexto (baritone guitar)

PARACHO, MICHOACÁN, MEXICO, c. 1985
Wood, metal, abalone
Marco Guerrero, maker
41 x 15⅜ x 4½ in.

This stunning guitar uses six pairs or "courses" of strings. Along with the accordion, the *bajo sexto* is a core component of conjunto music (Tex-Mex) in southern Texas and norteño music in northern Mexico, both of which feature musical elements of polka.

Cajun accordion
(button accordion)

EUNICE, LOUISIANA, USA, 2009
Wood, metal, cardstock
Marc Savoy, maker
13¼ x 13 x 7¼ in.

National Heritage Fellowship recipient
Marc Savoy made this beautiful accordion
just for MIM from rare Louisiana red pine,
salvaged from a Civil War-era building on
his family farm. The single-row, 10-button
accordion is an essential ingredient in
Cajun music.

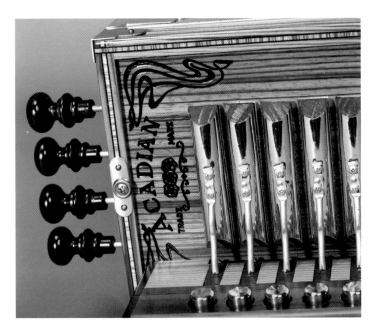

AFRICAN ARRIVALS
From Bondage to Musical Roots for a Nation

"Old Plantation" banjo (plucked lute)

BALTIMORE, MARYLAND, USA, 2009
Gourd, wood, animal skin
Peter R. Ross, maker
36 x 9 x 9 in.

This is a replica of a string instrument depicted in a late
18th-century watercolor known as *The Old Plantation*,
shown in the exhibit photo above. The anonymous artist
offers a glimpse into the leisure time of slaves in what
probably is South Carolina, while Pete Ross's meticulous
work brings to life one precursor of the modern banjo.

"Engraved Owens Mill Deluxe" banjo
(plucked lute)

STAUNTON, VIRGINIA, USA, 2009
Wood, metal, mother-of-pearl
Huss & Dalton Musical Instruments, maker
Ron Raymer, artist
38½ x 13½ x 4½ in.

Created especially for the MIM collection, this banjo contains elaborate carvings and engravings of tobacco leaves and flowers along the body and neck. The back of the instrument depicts the Owens Mill, a water-powered gristmill once located on the Dalton family's Virginia tobacco farm.

Mechanical-action pipe organ
INDIANAPOLIS, INDIANA, USA, 2009
White oak, walnut, Douglas fir, poplar,
ash, grenadilla, holly, and ebony woods;
lead, tin, aluminum, brass, iron; glass
Michael Rathke, maker
84 x 54 x 24 in.
Made possible through the support of
Floyd and Marie Ganassi

Offering a rare glimpse inside a pipe organ, the custom-built "visible organ" puts all exterior and interior mechanical and tone-producing portions of the instrument on display. With 183 pipes of varying lengths, the instrument includes special details such as hand-carved pipe shades and keys with a "reverse skunk tail" design—two pieces of light holly wood flanking a strip of dark ebony.

I Am AZ Music includes exhibits representing country stars **Marty Robbins and Buck Owens,** and jazz greats **Russell Moore and Charles Mingus.** Over 30 exhibits combine to celebrate Arizona's importance in the history of American music. *(Loans courtesy of John P. Dixon; Buck Owens' Crystal Palace, Bakersfield, CA; Huhugam Heritage Center, Gila River Indian Community)*

The Audio Recorders exhibit pays tribute to Floyd Ramsey's famed Phoenix recording studio. **Waylon Jennings, Lee Hazlewood, and Duane Eddy** each recorded at the studio and are featured in adjacent exhibits. *(Loans courtesy of John P. Dixon, Jerry Davis, Deke Dickerson, Clarke Rigsby, Floyd & Mary Ramsey, Tim Ramsey, and Jack Miller)*

The Canyon Records exhibit features awards and albums from one of the oldest independent record labels in the music industry. Canyon Records was founded more than 60 years ago and specializes in producing and distributing Native American music. *(Loan courtesy of Canyon Records)*

The Gin Blossoms and Alice Cooper exhibits showcase two Arizona-born bands that became international sensations. Guests can view a guitar belonging to original Gin Blossoms songwriter Doug Hopkins and two stage outfits made for Alice Cooper. *(Loans courtesy of Bill & Sandra Leen, John P. Dixon, and Alice Cooper)*

The Lalo Guerrero, Gilbert Velez, and Linda Ronstadt exhibits highlight the musical contributions of three Tucson-born artists. **The Stevie Nicks and Jordin Sparks exhibits** emphasize the achievements of two female vocalists from the Phoenix area. *(Loans courtesy of Mark Guerrero and Dan Guerrero, John P. Dixon, Manuel Velez and Gilbert Velez, University of Arizona School of Music, and Jordin Sparks)*

The Martin Workshop exhibit features acoustic guitars and tools used in the construction process.

The Hip Hop exhibit includes a drum machine, mixer, and two turntables—equipment that helped create signature sounds of the genre. Set in motion in the 1970s by African-American and Hispanic street culture in the Bronx, hip hop is now a global phenomenon.

(right) **The Big Drum exhibit** includes two examples of an instrument that originated in the Plains but now is at the heart of intertribal gatherings called "powwows" throughout North America.

Big Drum

Powwow time

Sabahpaki
(double-headed cylindrical drum)
Southern Plains people, Oklahoma,
USA, 2008.
Bull skin, bull sinew
Leonard Eschiti (Comanche), maker
played with stand.

Leg bells

Automaton music box from Germany (page 179)

Mechanical Music Gallery

The Mechanical Music gallery features a selection of musical instruments that, by definition, "play themselves." The gallery highlights a range of types and technologies, including artistic examples that feature animated components such as human and animal figures.

The rise and fall of the popularity of mechanical instruments is an engaging story that combines music, technology, commerce, and fashion.

Mechanical instruments may be powered by hand cranks, foot pumps, spring motors, electricity, or steam. They may rely on pneumatic hoses, mechanical gears, or electromagnetic components. All of them play music stored in some kind of binary format, making them the ancestors of digital computers. Their "software" comes in an ingenious array of barrels, cylinders, discs, paper rolls, cards, and folding books, and they are "programmed" with pins, teeth, or perforations. Some mechanical instruments are partially automated, requiring user input, like the "triola" mechanical zither (the player strums the bass strings) and the player piano (the operator adjusts the tempo, volume, and expression levers). Others are fully automated, like the cylinder music box and reproducing piano.

The Apollonia dance organ is one of the most popular instruments in MIM's collection and is played at the museum on a regular basis.

The idea of automating musical instruments is not recent. The earliest documented examples of automated bells and singing birds date from the first century. During the Middle Ages, bells in clock towers were automated by giant pinned cylinders. By about 1800, this idea had been scaled down to provide music boxes for home use.

Refinements and innovations multiplied over the next 130 years in what has been called the Golden Age of Mechanical Music, yielding a remarkable range of self-playing instruments from Europe and the Americas. This era stemmed from the fine craftsmanship of Swiss watch and clock makers, who made expensive luxury items for the well-to-do. Increasingly, in the nineteenth century, additional inventions and advancements in mass production made a variety of mechanical instruments more affordable. By the twentieth century, consumers around the world had

automatic music at their fingertips. For pleasure, worship, and study, these instruments filled streets, parks, ice-skating rinks, soda shops, dance halls, homes, and churches with traditional tunes, operatic melodies, symphonic excerpts, ethnic dances, and sacred hymns, to name a few.

This era also includes the invention of the phonograph—an analog rather than a digital device. For the first time in history, live music, including the human voice, could be recorded, packaged, and purchased. Eventually, this new era of high fidelity would bring the Golden Age of Mechanical Music to its close.

The rise and fall of the popularity of these machines is an engaging story that combines music, technology, commerce, and fashion. In MIM's Mechanical Music gallery, guests continue to enjoy the world of music these instruments store and play.

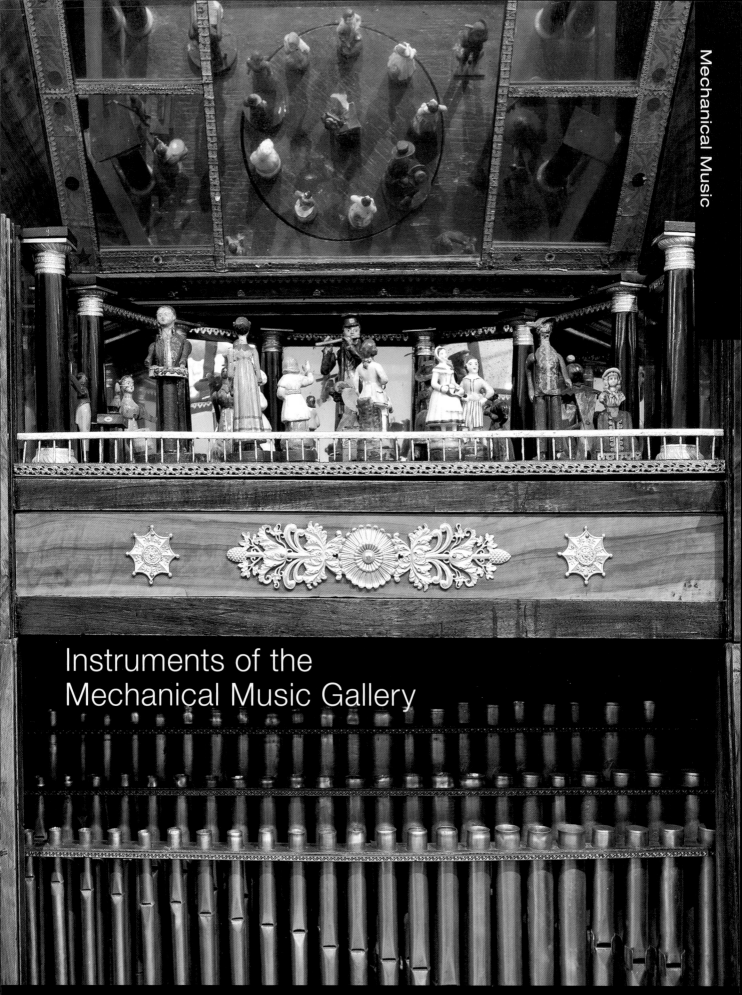

Instruments of the
Mechanical Music Gallery

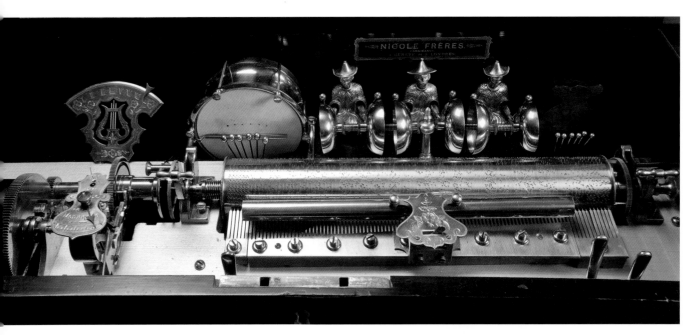

Orchestral music box

GENEVA, SWITZERLAND, c. 1903
Wood, brass, steel, chrome,
animal skin, felt
Nicole Frères, maker
39¼ x 12¾ x 16½ in. (music box)
44½ x 28½ x 24¼ in. (stand)
Gift of Rawhide Western Town

This instrument was made at
the height of cylinder music-box
production. It has all the "bells
and whistles," including a drum,
castanets, a mandolin effect,
and Mandarin figures striking
visible bells. The music box's
stand has a drawer for storing
extra cylinders.

Did You Know?
Due to their exceptional skills,
Swiss watchmakers were
the most famous artisans of
cylinder music boxes.

Bird box (automaton music box)
GERMANY, MID-20TH c.
Sterling silver, brass, steel, animal skin, feathers
4½ x 2 x 3 in.

Cog wheels and levers activate this music box's tiny bellows, giving breath to the bird's voice, and a slide-whistle mechanism produces a variable pitch that imitates birdsong.

Curator's Note
Automatons are figures that move mechanically and often have a musical component. They come in a variety of characters including a Turkish tea drinker, a French seamstress, and strolling pigs. Luxury collectibles were popular in the 19th century, when Parisian makers sold these small wonders around the world.

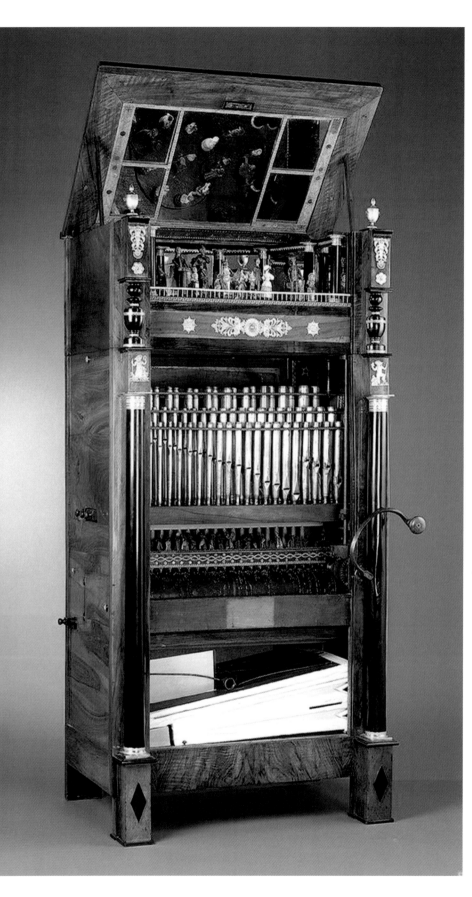

Orgue de salon
(automaton barrel organ)

FRANCE, 1790–1830
Wood, brass, ceramic, paper, glass,
animal skin
61 x 32½ x 23 in.

This soft-spoken salon
instrument is one of a kind, likely
made for a wealthy patron. Its
impressive tower was pieced
together from at least two
instruments dating from different
periods, primarily the automaton
section on top coupled with the
barrel organ on the bottom. The
composite instrument is housed
in a retrofitted neoclassical case
fit for a fashionable and well-to-
do salon.

Xorgan (barrel organ)

ODESSA, UKRAINE, c. 1910
Wood, brass, leather, textile,
chrome, nickel, plastic
Ivan Viktorovich Nechada, maker
23 x 20 x 14¼ in.

The bright tone and volume of this instrument are
well suited for playing outdoors. Despite its compact
size, this organ is one of the loudest instruments in
MIM's mechanical music collection.

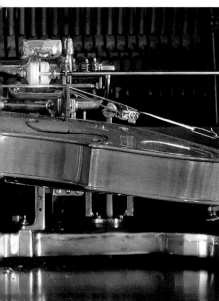

Violano Virtuoso
(mechanical violin and piano)

**CHICAGO, ILLINOIS, USA,
1910–1930**
Wood, brass, nickel, iron, spruce,
paper, steel, mother-of-pearl, plastic
Mills Novelty Co., maker
64⅜ x 42 x 30½ in.

The Violano Virtuoso is a mechanical
violin accompanied by half a player
piano that plays paper rolls. Perforations
in the roll tell the Violano which notes to
play. The violin operates mechanically
by solenoids, a special variety of
electromagnets. In the early 20th century,
coin-operated Violanos could be found
in soda shops and candy stores,
where they earned extra money for the
establishment while entertaining patrons.

Arranging piano and master perforator

BRONX, NEW YORK, USA, 1931
Wood, iron, brass, copper, ivory, ebony, paper, plastic, rubber, felt, glass
Starr Piano Co., and QRS Music Co., makers
67 5/16 x 112 5/8 x 35 7/16 in.
Loan courtesy of QRS Music Technologies, Inc.

To manufacture a player-piano roll, a skilled arranger first punches a master roll on an arranging piano. It is a slow process, requiring several hours to play through a two-minute song. QRS Music Company, the leading roll manufacturer in the 20th century, used this technology to produce arranged rolls when it abandoned hand-played rolls in 1931.

Curator's Note
Before electric recordings became commercially feasible in the late 1940s, player-piano rolls were arguably the best means to listen to high-fidelity music in the home.

PLAYER PIANOS

Rolmonica
(mechanical mouth organ)

BALTIMORE, MARYLAND, USA, LATE 1920s
Bakelite, wood, brass, chrome
Rolmonica Music Co., maker
2¾ x 5¼ x 3¾ in.

This instrument produces the same pitch on inhale and exhale; the operator only has to crank and blow.

Clarola (mechanical mouth organ)
CHICAGO, ILLINOIS, USA, c. 1930
Wood, plastic, metal, paper
Q.R.S. DeVry Corp., maker
13³⁄₁₆ x 3½ x 3¼ in.
Ex Fiske Collection, Claremont University Consortium

With notes that changed automatically and no need to learn a complex fingering system, this clarinet-shaped instrument was advertised as being extremely easy to play. Longtime Q.R.S. piano-roll arranger J. Lawrence Cook also made rolls for the Clarola.

Playasax (mechanical mouth organ)

CHICAGO, ILLINOIS, USA, c. 1930
Plastic, wood, paper, brass
Q.R.S. DeVry Corp., maker
11½ x 3½ x 5¼ in.

Like the Q.R.S. Clarola, the Playasax
was manufactured from the mid-1920s
to the 1930s.

Mechanical mouth organ

GERMANY, c. 1900
Brass, paper, felt
16½ x 3 x 6 in.

This mechanical harmonica is shaped like a trumpet.
Instruments like this, but of a bulkier design (eight-note
mechanical mouth organs), were first successfully sold
in the United States from the 1870s as "phonographic
cornets" and "trumpettos" during the organette craze.

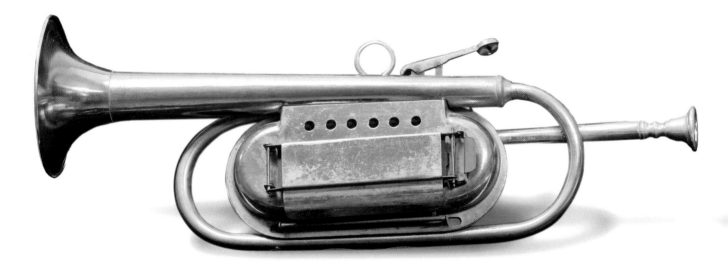

"Apollonia" dance organ (orchestrion)

ANTWERP, BELGIUM, 1926/1950

Wood, brass, steel, iron, nickel, rubber, copper, textile, plastic,
leather, felt

Theofiel Mortier, S.A., and Gebroeders Decap, makers

301¹⁵⁄₁₆ x 114 x 61⁷⁄₁₆ in.

The "Apollonia," made by two of the most famous
mechanical organ makers, is the largest and most
expensive instrument in MIM's permanent collection to
date. It is over 25 feet wide and has more than 680 organ
pipes, two accordions, two saxophones, a drum set, and
other percussion. The organ, which was once installed in
a 1950s Belgian dance hall, is again in the public domain
after having been in private hands for more than 20 years.

Curator's Note

When the "Apollonia" organ arrived at MIM, the staff had to maneuver the organ's largest central chest through the museum's corridors to reach the Mechanical Music gallery. When unpacked, the rest of the organ's multiple sections filled the entire 2,500 square feet of gallery space. It required six team members three full days to unpack, inspect, clean, and assemble them.

Music books

ANTWERP, BELGIUM, 1900–1950
Cardboard
Albert Decap, maker
Gebroeders Decap, maker
Urbain Van Wichelen, maker
6⅜ x 14¼ x 7½ in. ("Poet and Peasant")
6⅜ x 14¼ x 3 in. ("March Medley")
6⅜ x 14¼ x 1¼ in. ("Fox Trot")
6⅜ x 14¼ x 1¼ in. ("Fox Trot")
6⅜ x 14¼ x 1¼ in. ("Hi-Hi Twist Song")
6⅜ x 14¼ x 1¾ in. ("Yellow Rose of Texas")

These music books for the "Apollonia" dance organ are perforated cardboard, each containing one arranged tune or medley. Due to the long-standing popularity of mechanical dance organs, the music book repertoire includes a variety of genres, such as polka, swing, rumba, jazz, rock and roll, and even psychedelia. MIM's collection consists of 123 music books from a number of manufacturers and arrangers over decades of production.

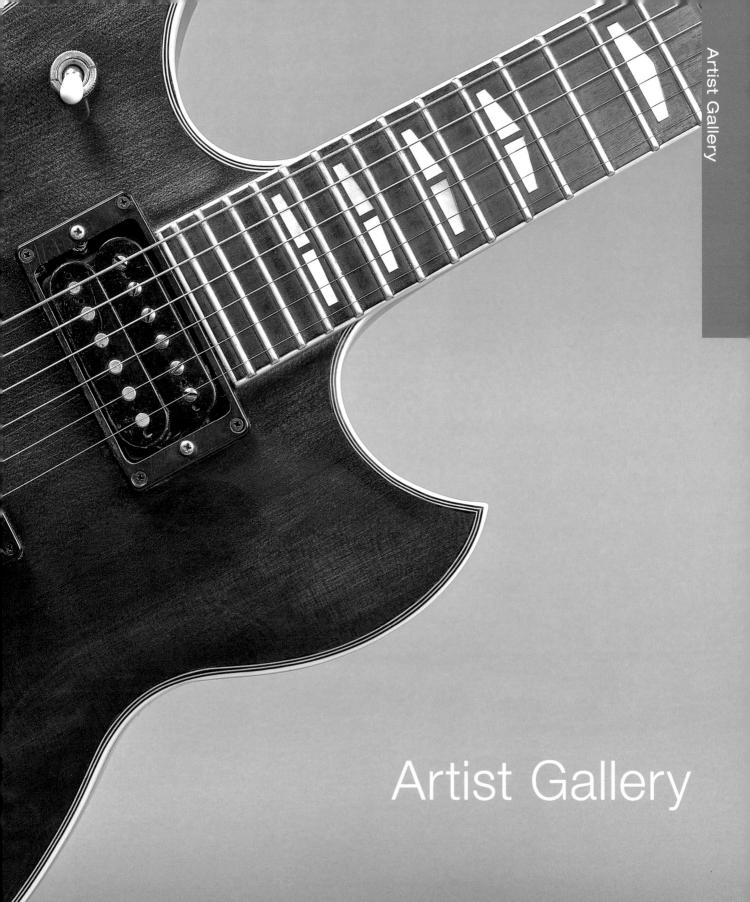

Artist Gallery

JOHN LENNON

Loan courtesy of
The Goss-Michael
Foundation

STEINWAY & SONS

Imagine

CARLOS SANTANA

The Carlos Santana exhibit showcases instruments used by the iconic guitarist throughout his inspired career, as well as the violin played by his father, José Santana. *(Loans courtesy of Carlos Santana and Irma Santana)*

(left) **The John Lennon Piano exhibit** contains the Steinway upright on which Lennon composed the song "Imagine," a famed appeal for peace. *(By kind permission of G. K. Panayiotou)*

The MIM Artist Gallery tells the stories of the world's great music makers, showcasing the iconic instruments they played.

In every time, place, and culture, a few select musical artists attain the highest level of renown. Their music touches the hearts of everyday people and wins approval from critics and connoisseurs. Over the course of their careers, gifted artists often forge a special relationship with a particular musical instrument, many of which are works of art themselves, exquisitely wrought and ingeniously designed. Some of the instruments even become celebrities in their own right—instantly recognizable and much beloved by fans.

The Dick Dale exhibit features instruments used and inspired by Dale as well as a custom-built Hansen surfboard—a symbol of his status as the "King of Surf Guitar." *(Loan courtesy of Dick Dale Enterprises)*

The MIM Artist Gallery tells the stories of the world's great music makers, showcasing the iconic instruments they played, along with compelling video footage, photographs, stage attire, and personal artifacts that help to bring these musical legends to life. The gallery is ever-changing, as instruments and other artifacts borrowed for display from legendary performers are returned and replaced by objects from other iconic artists and instrument makers.

Popular music is always well represented in this dynamic environment, with instruments on which artists such as John Lennon, Eric Clapton, Elvis Presley, Carlos Santana, and others have made musical history. Fascinating instruments from nationally and internationally known musicians such as King Sunny Adé, Eddie Palmieri, Savia Andina, Mahmoud Effat, R. Carlos Nakai, and Simon Shaheen are also featured, reflecting MIM's mission to foster, preserve, and celebrate global musical traditions.

Renowned instrument makers also get their due with places of honor in the Artist Gallery: from Henrich Engelhard Steinweg (Steinway), who founded a piano dynasty, to Avedis Zildjian, whose cymbals became known throughout the world. The gallery honors other key contributors to our musical heritage, too, with artifacts as varied as a baton wielded by maestro Leonard Bernstein and a microphone rocked by pop diva Rihanna. Also featured are musical instruments that have acquired fame through association with a historic occasion, such as a large, ornate Chinese drum used in the opening ceremonies of the 2008 Olympic Games in Beijing.

Diverse and intriguing, the exhibits in the MIM Artist Gallery commemorate those special moments when creativity meets craftsmanship, forging sounds that have marked history and moved and inspired millions of people all around the world.

Instruments of the Artist Gallery

Steve Vai's Ibanez triple-neck guitar (page 196)

Eric Clapton: "Stratocaster"
(electric guitar)

FULLERTON, CALIFORNIA, USA, 1956
Alder and maple woods, metal, plastic
Fender Musical Instruments Corporation, maker
39 x 13½ x 2½ in.
Loan courtesy of EMP Museum

Known in the 1960s as a member of
various bands including the Yardbirds
and Cream, Eric Clapton launched a
solo career in the 1970s. This Fender
Stratocaster, purchased in London in 1967
and given the nickname "Brownie," is the
guitar heard on early Clapton classics
such as "Layla" and "Bell Bottom Blues."

The Eric Clapton exhibit features two guitars
played by Clapton during his career: "Brownie" and
a Gibson ES-345TD electric guitar. Clapton favored
the Gibson models during his 1966–1968 tenure
with Cream. *(Loans courtesy of EMP Museum and
Jeffery C. Covill)*

Jake Shimabukuro:
Tenor ukulele (plucked lute)

HONOLULU, HAWAII, USA, 2009
Koa wood, rosewood, mahogany
Kamaka Hawaii, Inc., maker
27¼ x 7¾ x 2¼ in.
Gift of Jake Shimabukuro

Jake Shimabukuro has proven that the ukulele accommodates many musical styles including classical, rock, and jazz. During a January 2010 concert in Phoenix, Shimabukuro spoke about MIM and gave a moving performance of "Ave Maria" on the ukulele seen here. He then donated the instrument to the MIM collection with the request, "Please take good care of her."

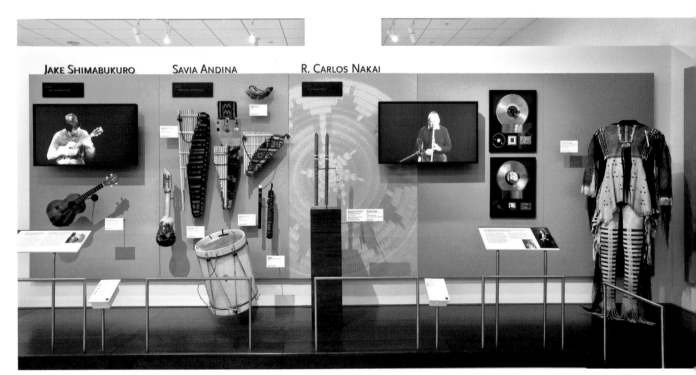

MIM Artist Gallery exhibits celebrate musical giants around the world—the artists who inspire and the remarkable symbols of musical history that they create. A few shown here include ukulele virtuoso Jake Shimabukuro, Bolivian folk group Savia Andina, and Native American flute master R. Carlos Nakai. *(Loan courtesy of R. Carlos Nakai)*

G.I. Piano

**QUEENS, NEW YORK,
NEW YORK, USA, 1945**
Walnut, lacquer, plastic, ebony,
metal, brass, felt
Steinway & Sons, maker
42⅛ x 58¼ x 23¹³⁄₁₆ in.
*Loan courtesy of Steinway &
Sons–America*

During World War II, most
instrument manufacture was
halted, but Steinway obtained
official permission to produce one
plucky model: the G.I. piano. Over
2,500 of these rugged, compact
instruments were sold to the U.S.
government starting in 1942.
Some were even parachuted into
the frontlines in the battlefields of
Europe to help boost the soldiers'
morale. This one is among the
few G.I. pianos that remain.

Steve Vai: Ibanez triple neck
(electric guitar)

LOS ANGELES, CALIFORNIA, USA, 1993
Alder, maple, and rosewood; metal
Hoshino (U.S.A.) Inc., maker
Pedro Cruz, artist
38¼ x 20¾ x 3 in.
Loan courtesy of Steve Vai

A true guitar virtuoso, Steve Vai endows
his music with imagination, passion, and a
remarkable mastery of technique. Vai composed
the piece "I Know You're Here" to be played on
this fanciful triple-neck guitar. The instrument has
been featured in concert, on television, and in
numerous publications.

Elvis Presley: D-28 (guitar)

NAZARETH, PENNSYLVANIA, USA, 1975
Indian rosewood, spruce, mahogany, and ebony;
metal; celluloid
C. F. Martin & Co., maker
41 x 15⁹⁄₁₆ x 4 in.
*Loan courtesy of Elvis Presley Enterprises, Inc.
"Graceland"*

Discovered in a Graceland closet in 1982, this is the last guitar on which Elvis Presley performed. The MIM conservation team treated a crack in the neck and several splits in the body, thereby restoring the instrument to the state in which it left Presley's hands following his last concert performance on June 26, 1977. The belt buckle scratches remain.

The Elvis Presley exhibit showcases important pieces of the King of Rock 'n' Roll's history in music and film. The exhibit includes two of his famous jumpsuits, two guitars, and other items from his storied career. *(Loan courtesy of Elvis Presley Enterprises, Inc. "Graceland")*

Simon Shaheen: 'Ūd (plucked lute)
DAMASCUS, SYRIA, 1926
Wood, mother-of-pearl
Antun Nahat, maker
31½ x 14¼ x 8¼ in.

'*Ūds* made by Antun Nahat are counted among the world's finest. This exquisite example was owned and played for many years by celebrated composer and virtuoso Simon Shaheen.

The Clara Rockmore exhibit features a theremin (an electronic instrument controlled by the player's hand movements in the air around two antennae), a diamond-shaped speaker, and a performance robe, each belonging to the late theremin virtuosa. Rockmore received this instrument in 1929 as a gift from its inventor, Lev Sergeyevich Termen (Léon Theremin). *(Loan courtesy of the family of Clara Rockmore.)*

John Denver: Guitar
KALAMAZOO, MICHIGAN, USA, EARLY 20TH c.
Wood, metal, plastic, mother-of-pearl
Gibson Mandolin-Guitar Mfg. Co., maker
39 x 14½ x 4½ in.
Loan courtesy of the John Denver Estate

Singer-songwriter John Denver won admiration from audiences around the world. A childhood gift from his grandmother, this guitar was so special to Denver that he experienced a sense of grief upon its loss. After reuniting with the instrument years later, Denver composed "This Old Guitar" in 1974 to celebrate his long lost "friend."

The Zildjian exhibit features a model of the almost four-centuries-old cymbal-making process and a "Master Touch" drum kit built for Louie Bellson by Remo, Inc., outfitted with Zildjian cymbals. *(Loan courtesy of Avedis Zildjian Company)*

Buck Owens: Silvertone model 319
(electric acoustic guitar)

CHICAGO, ILLINOIS, USA, 1970–1971
Birch and spruce woods, metal, celluloid
Harmony Guitar Co., maker
41 x 15¼ x 4½ in.
Loan courtesy of Buck Owens' Crystal Palace, Bakersfield, CA

Known for helping to create the driving "Bakersfield Sound" in country music, singer and guitarist Buck Owens also was a television star. He often performed on this signature red-white-and-blue guitar as host of *The Buck Owens Ranch Show* and cohost of *Hee Haw.*

Did You Know?
The "Buck Owens American," an economical version of the red-white-and-blue guitar that Buck Owens played, was sold in the Sears & Roebuck catalog in the early 1970s. Sears previously had sold guitars inspired by Gene Autry, Roy Rogers, and other celebrities.

The George Benson exhibit features the artist's vintage Gibson "Johnny Smith," the main guitar used during the recording of his album *Breezin'*. Also on display is the 1976 GRAMMY Benson won for "This Masquerade." *(Loan courtesy of George Benson)*

The Sennheiser: Rockin' the Mic exhibit contains microphones representative of those used by some of today's preeminent vocalists such as Vince Neil, Hayley Williams, Seal, Rihanna, and Nelly Furtado. *(Loan courtesy of Sennheiser Electronic Corporation)*

(right) **The Olympic Drum exhibit** features drum number 18 of the 2,008 drums used during the opening ceremonies of the 2008 Summer Olympics in Beijing. This instrument was inspired by the ancient Chinese *fou*—a drum constructed from a wine vessel. *(Loan courtesy of Bowen Nian)*

OLYMPIC DRUM

Loan courtesy of
Bowen Nian

MAHMOUD EFFAT

Fou (square drum)
China, 2008

Loan courtesy of Bowen Nian

Conservation Lab

Experience Gallery

MIM Music Theater (Kronos Quartet performing)

Target Gallery

Museum Store

More of the MIM Experience

MIM's visible lab allows guests an unparalleled glimpse into the fascinating work of instrument conservation, something that is done behind the scenes in other museums.

Stewardship and interpretation of the collection are key missions of the museum.

Seen through a large viewing window, MIM's Conservation Lab gives guests a behind-the-scenes look at musical-instrument conservators at work. These specialists stabilize, clean, and sometimes restore objects from MIM's vast collection and prepare them for exhibition—all in full view of the public.

Stewardship and interpretation of the collection are key missions of the museum. Conservators' efforts to achieve these goals can be divided into two categories: preventive conservation and active conservation.

Preventive conservation addresses the needs of the collection as a whole and includes the control of environmental factors that influence the lifespan of museum objects, such as temperature, humidity, light, and pollution.

(Above) A MIM conservator works on Elvis Presley's Martin D-28. By the time this guitar was discovered at Graceland in 1982, it had suffered damage and undergone repair work that needed to be corrected. MIM was selected to perform this restoration.

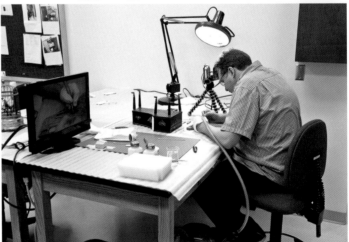

Integrated pest management is another important aspect of preventive conservation. At MIM, all incoming objects that can be subjected to low temperatures are placed in the museum's walk-in freezer for a period of more than seventy-two hours to kill any potentially harmful insects, larvae, and eggs. To monitor the entry of living insects and pests into the galleries and collection areas, conservators set "sticky traps" and refresh them once a month. They then count and identify all insects found on the traps. If a high number of a species dangerous to the collection is found, the Conservation Department identifies the source and eliminates the problem.

Active conservation procedures aim to stabilize the construction or surface elements of an individual instrument.

The simple act of cleaning an instrument is an important task—not just because it improves aesthetic appeal, but also because it removes dust that attracts humidity and serves as a nutrient medium for biological activity.

Active conservation also involves examining the objects and sometimes replacing missing or damaged elements such as strings or bridges with appropriate substitutes. This often requires research into historical construction techniques. In addition to archival research, conservators examine the objects themselves. Their findings inform the selection of required treatments and contribute to curatorial knowledge. With this highly technical and specialized work, MIM's conservators participate in "interpreting" the instruments and in making them accessible and interesting to the public.

MIM's unique Experience Gallery invites guests of all ages to touch, play, and hear a changing array of instruments from many different cultures.

Bang a gong, strum a Burmese harp, and play instruments from all corners of the world. MIM's unique Experience Gallery invites guests of all ages to touch, play, and hear a changing array of instruments from many different cultures.

Some of the instruments are familiar; others are not. But as guests experience the different ways instruments are made, and explore the different ways instruments are played, they learn how sound is affected by size, shape, and material, and they discover the amazing diversity of sounds they themselves can create.

A nickelodeon, a theremin, a harp from Paraguay, and a large gong from Indonesia—these are just a few of the instruments in the Experience Gallery. Talking drums from Nigeria, rain sticks from Chile, a marimba from Zimbabwe, gamelan instruments from Java, and a *panghyang* from South Korea—there are dozens more to discover.

Whether guests play on their own or are accompanied by family, friends, or complete strangers, guests in the Experience Gallery do more than have fun trying their hand at new instruments. They participate in music being dramatically brought to life and connect with others sharing the experience. Together, their imaginations catch fire in this inspired musical world that encourages and celebrates the musician within each of us.

Guests do more than have fun trying their hand at new instruments. They participate in music being dramatically brought to life.

TARGET GALLERY

American Sabor: Latinos in U.S. Popular Music was the first traveling exhibition to be featured at MIM.
It opened in the Target Gallery on November 20, 2010.

Exhibits in the Target Gallery enrich guests' musical journey and foster an appreciation for cultures around the world.

The Target Gallery houses temporary displays, traveling exhibitions, and other special shows at MIM. Nearly 2,700 square feet in area, this exhibit space was developed with the help of a grant from Target Corporation.

American Sabor: Latinos in U.S. Popular Music, a traveling exhibition from the EMP Museum in Seattle, Washington, opened the gallery in November 2010. The show traced the influence of Latin American musicians on North American popular music and culture.

The *SANZA: African Thumb Pianos* exhibition displayed thumb pianos of various shapes, types, and sizes. It opened in the Target Gallery on February 25, 2012.

This was followed by *The Power of Music: Photographic Portraits of Americans and Their Musical Instruments, 1860–1915*. Filled with sixty 24 x 36 in. photographs, tintypes, *cartes de visite*, cabinet cards, and other beguiling sepia-toned images of people posing with their musical instruments, this exhibition took MIM guests to the turbulent, fast-changing period bracketed by the Civil War and World War I. Paired with the photos were rare instruments from MIM's own American collection, selected to match as closely as possible the instruments in the photos.

SANZA: African Thumb Pianos from the Collections of F. & F. Boulanger-Bouhière and MIM was the next exhibition in the Target Gallery. Featuring two hundred thumb pianos on loan from a private Belgian collection, as well as those from MIM's own collection (including loans from the Royal Museum for Central Africa), the exhibition presented a range of thumb-piano styles brought to life with accompanying audio and video recordings.

Opening on September 24, 2011, *The Power of Music* traveling exhibition offered guests a glimpse into an amazing age for music.

Whatever exciting and informative exhibitions come to the Target Gallery in the future, they will be sure to complement MIM's vast permanent collection and comprehensive mission. The exhibits in the Target Gallery will enrich guests' musical journey and foster an appreciation for cultures around the world.

The Target Gallery houses temporary displays, traveling exhibitions, and other special shows at MIM.

The Preservation Hall Jazz Band

Jeremy Denk

Joshua Bell

Suzy Bogguss

The 300-seat theater was designed to give concertgoers an extraordinary, intimate experience.

MIM's mission is to bring to life the world's musical instruments, and there is no better way to do this than through dynamic live performances in the MIM Music Theater, a spectacular venue that hosts an eclectic range of concerts by global artists.

The three-hundred-seat theater was designed to give concertgoers an extraordinary, intimate experience. Architecturally striking, the theater spans two floors of the museum, its low stone walls, wooden proscenium, and stone-colored maple-wood stage evoking the rocks of Arizona canyons. But the design is not only aesthetically appealing; the architecture isolates the theater physically and acoustically from the rest of the museum.

The superb acoustics and beautiful setting provide an unparalleled, up-close-and-personal experience for audience and performers alike. A premier destination, the MIM Music Theater has attracted leading artists from across the country and around the world—from *American Idol* winner Jordin Sparks to jazz legend Ahmad Jamal to master of the Ghanaian *gyil* Bernard Woma. Indeed, reflecting MIM's goal to highlight the diversity of cultures and global musical practices, the theater has already hosted performers from more than thirty countries.

In addition to featuring both well-known performers and exciting new talents onstage, the MIM Music Theater offers workshops, films, lectures, and interactive performances that draw guests deeper into musical trends and traditions.

Moreover, the MIM Music Theater was designed to be an optimal recording space. It boasts top-of-the-line recording equipment and handpicked concert instruments, including a Steinway Model D grand piano tuned especially for the space. Other highlights include a Yamaha Recording Custom drum kit and an impressive selection of microphones. As an added vote of confidence, Sony recorded Grammy-winning violinist Joshua Bell and acclaimed pianist Jeremy Denk's *French Impressions* CD at MIM in 2010, the first commercial album recorded at the MIM Music Theater.

Paquito D'Rivera and the Brasil Guitar Duo

k.d. lang

The Café at
MIM offers
a menu that
changes
daily, boasting
dishes alive
with freshness
and flavor.

Located in a light-filled space overlooking the *Phoenix* sculpture and the museum's main courtyard, the award-winning Café at MIM serves an inventive array of great-tasting, thoughtfully prepared foods made from scratch using fresh, local ingredients. These dishes, along with the café's relaxed environment and inviting courtyard, provide a unique museum dining experience.

In an extension of the philosophy exhibited throughout the museum, the Café at MIM takes a comprehensive view of food, believing that environment, community, and a creative menu work together to contribute to the well-being and enjoyment of guests.

The Café at MIM offers a menu that changes daily, boasting dishes alive with freshness and flavor. Stations feature global cuisine, local and regional dishes, hand-tossed pizzas, grilled specialties, soups and salads, kid-friendly fare, and delicious desserts. Adjacent to the Café is the MIM Coffee Shop, serving beverages, pastries, and quick snacks.

The Museum Store presents a wide selection of items that educate, entertain, and inspire.

Just inside the museum, across from MIM's main entrance, the Museum Store presents a wide selection of items that educate, entertain, and inspire. The store sells a variety of books for adults and children about the music and cultures of the world. Guests can also find familiar and unusual musical instruments, ranging from pieces built by master instrument makers to those made under fair-trade conditions by artisans around the world to simple, fun, and affordable favorites. Add on CDs, jewelry, housewares, and more, and the Museum Store is sure to have something for every guest.

There is no admission required to shop at the Museum Store, and proceeds help support MIM and its programs.

MIM: Highlights from the Musical Instrument Museum

Edited by Karen Werner
Assistant editor: Brian Dredla
Copy editor: Sunny Benitez-Rush

Photographed by Jacqueline Byers
Photo assistant: Linda Kirsh

All photos by Jacqueline Byers with the exception of:

- Shannon Brinkman, p. 210 (top)

- Jimmy C. Carrauthers, p. 2 (top right), p. 13 (top left, top right, and bottom)

- ©MIM, p. 6 (bottom), p. 21, p. 54 (bottom), p. 153 (bottom), p. 157 (bottom right), pgs. 172-173, p. 179, p. 186 (bottom), p. 197 (bottom), p. 205 (top), p. 208, p. 212 (top left, center left, bottom center, and bottom right)

- Courtesy of Mark Gardner, Cascade, Colorado, p. 209 (bottom)

- Christine Keith, p. 13 (top center)

- Lisa Marie Mazzucco, p. 210 (center right)

- Photo courtesy of EMP Museum, p. 194 (right)

- Photo courtesy of Marty and Elise Roenigk/ Mechantique, p. 180 (left)

- Daniel C. Piper, front endpapers

- P.S. Studios, p. 123, p. 175, p. 182 (top left and bottom)

- Bruce Racine, p. 2 (top center), p. 6 (top left), p. 7 (top right and bottom), p. 9, p. 12 (bottom left), p. 174, p. 176, p. 202 (top right), p. 204 (top right and bottom right), p. 206 (left and top right), p. 207 (top left and bottom right)

- Matthew Rood, p. 210 (bottom), p. 211 (top and bottom left)

- Dennis Scully, D Squared Productions, Inc., pgs. 202-203 (bottom)

- Craig Smith, p. 194 (left)

- Cullen B. Strawn, back endpapers

- Bill Timmerman, back cover (bottom), pgs. 2-3 (bottom), p. 4 (left), p. 11 (bottom left), p. 12 (bottom right), p. 212 (top right and bottom left), p. 215

- Michael Wilson, p. 210 (center left)

- www.bradreedphotography.com, p. 211 (bottom right)

Designed by P.S. Studios, Inc.
Printed by Ben Franklin Press

MIM wishes to thank the additional team members, past and present, and consultants who contributed to the research, writing, and photographing of this book. Their expertise and assistance are greatly appreciated.

Editorial Team
Christopher Bell
Sara Blackwood
Bill DeWalt, PhD
Alan di Perna
Karen Farugia
Marc Felix
Sylvia Keller
Holly Metz
Jennifer Post, PhD
April Salomon
Peter Shikany
Robert Ulrich
John Werner
and the MIM Exhibits and
    Multimedia Department Team

Curatorial Team
Manuel Jordán, PhD,
    *Chief Curator and
    Director of Collections*

Christina Linsenmeyer, PhD
Cullen B. Strawn, PhD
Daniel C. Piper, PhD
Colin Pearson
Clint Spell
David Wegehaupt
Emily Ham
Brian Dredla

Conservation Team
Irene Peters
    Head of Conservation

Daniel Heath Cull
Adriana Milinic
Jill Crane

*Registration and Collections
Management Team*
Katie Anderson, *Head of Registration
    and Collections Management*

Anna Bierne
Erin Donovan
Linda Kirsh
Jennifer Rogers
Steve Hinders
Cristina Caballero
Frank J. Gonzales
Troy Sharp